W9-BZR-603

Daughter in Retrograde

Daughter in Retrograde

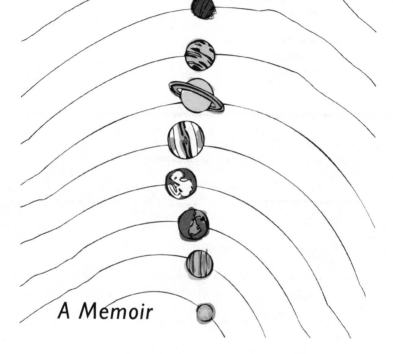

A Memoir

Courtney Kersten

The University of Wisconsin Press

Publication of this book has been made possible, in part, through support from the **Brittingham Trust.**

The University of Wisconsin Press
1930 Monroe Street, 3rd Floor
Madison, Wisconsin 53711-2059
uwpress.wisc.edu

3 Henrietta Street, Covent Garden
London WCE 8LU, United Kingdom
eurospanbookstore.com

Printed in the United States of America

This book may be available in a digital edition.

Library of Congress Cataloging-in-Publication Data

Names: Kersten, Courtney, author.
Title: Daughter in retrograde: a memoir / Courtney Kersten.
Description: Madison, Wisconsin: The University of Wisconsin Press, [2018]
Identifiers: LCCN 2017042906 | ISBN 9780299317003 (cloth: alk. paper)
Subjects: LCSH: Kersten, Courtney. | Authors, American—21st century—
    Biography. | Astrologers—United States—Biography.
Classification: LCC PS3611.E777 Z46 2018 | DDC 813/.6 [B]—dc23
LC record available at https://lccn.loc.gov/2017042906

Events, locales, and conversations have been recreated from the author's memories of them. Certain names and identifying details of persons and places have been changed to protect their identity.

For my mother,
who told us to laugh about it

And for my brother,
who reminded me

Partial truth—the seeds of wisdom—can be found in many places . . . in earthly law, social custom, scientific research, philosophy and religious doctrines . . . in art, music and poetry . . . and, above all, in Nature. But real Truth can be found in one place only—in every man's and woman's communion with an eternal Source of hidden Knowledge within—which each individual must seek and find for himself or herself. We may point out the path to others, but each must walk along that path alone—until every single "lost one" has made the whole journey.

Linda Goodman, *Love Signs*

Retrograde (ˈre•trəˌgrād)
adjective
    1. a body, on earth, in space, moving backwards
noun
    1. metamorphosis triggered by inescapable self-examination
    2. an illusion

Contents

**Part Three:
Retrograde Direct Station**

**Part Four:
Post-Retrograde Shadow**

Prologue

The Axis Point

Your Reading For: March 17, 2012

Despite your splashing in the so-called Deep End of all things mystical and woo-woo, there is only so much you can know, young one. Today is a midwestern fantasy—middle of March and 82 degrees. What other magic do you need? Relish this heat, young sprite. The ultimate goal is presence, not prediction.

A woman sunbathes on her blacktop driveway. The sun beats down on her, turning those spray-tanned shoulders and thighs pink as the lawn chair she's splayed out on. Two hollow beer bottles sit next to her as she slides her cat-eye sunglasses up her nose. She's wearing that zebra-print bikini she found on sale back in November and has been waiting to wear since. Look in this woman's closet and you'll see her other treasures—she's been scouring the bathing suit sale racks since last September. Look in her medicine cabinet and you're not going to find any herbal supplements or glucosamine for her creaky knees. You're going to find bottle after bottle of spray tan and crusty bronzing lotion collected for the past decade. Look at her again— were you fooled? Do you believe that she's been living here, in This Place of snow and silence and sunlessness, for the past five months? Or is she someone else—someone who's just visiting this rural Wisconsin pocket of a town?

Crane your neck, look just past her into the lawn, and her cover is blown—the remnants of her abound. Snow's still melting in a dirty heap where she and her daughter lazily shoveled it after a

December storm. You can't see it, but they carved their initials into that icy lump. Turn to the left and there's a stray fleece glove abandoned in the lawn that looks like it just might fit her delicate hand. Look at her right ankle. Zoom in on her lower shin you'll see the blue bruise where a hairline fracture festers. She slipped on the ice two weeks ago and it's ached ever since.

Yeah—she's local.

Look to the west and it's all lakes and white pine forests until you hit the Minnesota border. Look to the east and it's rolling farmland and Holstein dairy cows until you wade into Lake Michigan. Look beyond that woman's toes and you'll see her home: a humble, hunter-green A-frame house with white shutters that sits beside a lake of six thousand acres. She grew up on this lake and knows the rivers and streams that branch off from it. She knows the way it collects algae and seaweed in the summer and the way it turns frozen and overrun with ice fishing shacks during the winter. She knows the way a white pine looks when you're lying flat on your back staring up through the branches. She knows what it feels like to live in this climate of extremes—between the never-ending snow and humid summer, the calico fall and sopping spring, the gaping silences and fervent gossip. Look just north of her and you'll see her ninety-year-old neighbor, Moses Sperling, dressed in a down coat and wool hat standing before a burn barrel where he sets his trash aflame each afternoon, letting a nasty funk loose in this lakeside neighborhood that'll stink until sunset. How does he always manage to park his barrel right on the edge of the property line?

Look back at her as she turns the page in her thick paperback novel and you'll see the bubblegum scar tracing her left breast from a lumpectomy sixteen years earlier. She's fifty-six now and back then she underwent experimental treatment, double the rounds of radiation and drugs dripped into her veins that's common practice today at half-dose.

But, look closer. Study her. See the way her heart-shaped face intently reads that page? See the way she smirks at the end of the chapter? See the way she smooths those blonde bangs off her forehead? Look even closer—observe the speckles of gold in her green eyes, those silver fillings in her back molars, the bubbling flesh on her elbow from when a boyfriend thrust her into the street at age sixteen. Now look beyond all that—can you see it? Can you see those rebellious cells that lurk within her? The clues of her imminent demise? The trail of crumbs that leads to her ultimate end?

Of course not. Because she can't see it either.

Nobody's looking at those blood cells turning rogue within her. Not a soul is thinking about that radiation sixteen years ago now betraying the body it once saved. Nobody is aware that in this very moment she's living on the eve of the last year of her life. How could she know? How could anyone know? And even if she did know, if it had been transcribed to her in a telegram from beyond or spelled out in the steam from her coffee cup, would she believe it?

Probably not—who would want to believe that?

Zoom out and look at the end of the driveway. No, it's not a mirage—there's some girl with a scowl on her face clomping down it. She's got on some stained polyester navy blue suit that's two sizes too big. She's wearing those clunky orthopedic office shoes she found at the thrift store for four bucks. She's a boomerang kid; a twenty-three-year-old with a penchant for impulsively buying plane tickets abroad, blowing through her meager cash, and then crawling back home again homesick and broke. Look in her passport and she's spent the past few years bouncing back and forth— mostly between Latvia and the Upper Midwest. Look in her recent past and she just got back—she thought living in southern Italy for the Wisconsin winter would be grand until she ran out of money and ended up living off stale bread and rice until she could catch a ride home. She just got back from her recently acquired morning shift at the local derelict hotel where she works the desk.

Look back at the woman on the lawn chair as recognition wafts across her face—yeah, that's her daughter walking down the driveway. Look back at the girl in that hideous suit—yeah, that's her mother sunbathing down there.

Look above both of them and it's all blue sky and sun. It's kites flying and pollen sprinting on the wind. But look past that. Go beyond the bulbous clouds of the troposphere and get into the stratosphere's atmospheric flows. Observe the hot air balloons.

Look at that layer of ozone you just crossed. Then go further— traverse the shooting stars of the mesosphere, gaze at a meteor, and hang out beyond the auroras of the thermosphere. Let their beauty astound you. Take a few more steps and a series of celestial bodies will come into clear view. It's our solar system. Catch your breath and look at that moon, at Venus and Mercury glowing. Pivot around to gaze at Mars' ruddy face or that expansive surface of Jupiter or the rings of Saturn. Pull out the binoculars and squint at those distant bodies—Uranus, Neptune, and the stars beyond. Now, stay there for a moment. Close your eyes and breathe. Let your mind go blank. Surrounded by those celestial bodies, does anything float across your mind? An image from the past, a message, or a sign?

Look back to those women, to the mother and daughter now both sunbathing on the driveway. That girl has stripped down to her underwear and splayed her honey-hued body out beside her mother. Though they can't see with clarity to the heights of the thermosphere or hang out with those planets, they've certainly pondered them. These women spend their time splashing around in the so-called Deep End of mysticism, astrology, and signs from beyond. It's one of their hobbies.

Listen to the daughter chatter about taking apart that copy machine at work and to her mother recap her morning shift at the local hospital where she's a nurse. Listen to them talk and talk until that girl passes out in her underwear, taken under by the weight of waking up at 4 a.m. to prepare for the early shift. That girl lying there, she's been thinking about those planets for years—the transits of Jupiter, the messages of Saturn, the metaphors of Venus. Does she know about those cells turning rogue? About the radiation turning her mother's body toxic? About the fact that the woman she feels closest to, the woman who is the axis point of her universe, will be gone within months?

No, she's not thinking about any of that. But if she were to look back at the happenings of the past maybe she'd tie a string and connect one instance to another. And maybe then she'd see the signs and patterns. Maybe then she'd see that inevitable path. But if we were to do that—to tell a story about a mother and a daughter, about faith and doubt—we'd have to look back further than this moment sunbathing in the driveway. We'd have to look at the decades and days of years past. We'd have to start with this—that woman there in the zebra bikini is my mother, Victoria.

And that girl? That girl is me.

Part One

The Retrograde Pre-Shadow

The celestial body progresses forward; routine,
normalcy, intermittent upset.

Tarot

Your Reading For: January 2, 1998

Well, well, baby Ram! Diving right in, aren't we? While it may be easier to ignore those feelings of apprehension remember that just because you have the ability to ask doesn't mean that the answers will always be pleasant.

At first glance, this is just another one of those townie taverns where the cigarette smoke hovers so thick that you wear it on your nylon winter coat until the wind at Monday's lunchtime recess finally blows that eau-de-Friday-night-funk out of its fibers. This is another bar with a cardboard cutout of Brett Favre posed in his Packer jersey next to a fire extinguisher against wood-paneled walls. This is another one of those Wisconsin watering holes decorated with whitetail racks covered in Christmas tree lights nailed to the wall. Below the antlers, the slot machines blink as my mother shoves coin after coin into them. Wearing a red cashmere sweater, high-waisted black jeans, and gold hoops, a flurry of sprayed dishwater blonde curls crown her. Sticking quarters into the Crazy Diamonds, she watches the reels turn, holds her breath as she hopes for three sensual bunches of cherries to meet in the middle, and slaps the rim of the machine when they don't. Her eyebrows arch as she watches her credits disappear before feverishly digging in her purse for more change. And for anyone but me and my seven-year-old brother Donny, she's just another woman dressed up to go out on a Friday night. And this is just another one of those places you pass by on the highway, miserable and dumpy and lonely looking in the daylight, where they play Van

Halen and Heart and jukebox one-hit wonders and half the neon lights blinking above the bar have burnt out so what was previously "Dick's Chalet" is now "Di   et."

But even at nine years old, as I spin on the red pleather barstools by the KISS pinball machine, I know that this is a place where we are privy to an alternate reality. To me, this bar is a sacred place where people speak something close to the truth; it's like a police station. I know that this is where you need to listen up because the words slurred by our parents and adults across bar stools and in between sips or puffs are quite possibly the real truth—or it's at least unfiltered, earnest, and heartfelt, which is better than anything else we hear. Because everything outside this bar is a theater, a performance of the social nuances, codes, and expectations of This Place where what you say onstage may not be the person you are offstage.

And that's where things begin to get muddled.

In This Place, friendliness is an ethical issue. I call it "This Place" because it's not only a location but a culture anybody born here carries with them. Here, to be publicly unfriendly, saturnine, or simply aloof is as uncalled for as leaving flaming piles of dog crap on a childhood enemy's doorsteps or setting a pasture of dairy cows free for your own entertainment. You stink. And we can smell it. The funk of being that cashier that didn't smile or the dude at the gas station who kept to himself is something people remember in This Place. It's not minding your own business or having a bad day or respecting "boundaries." Boundaries? What are those? Friendliness is like winter. Friendliness is like taxes. Friendliness *is*. And failure to comply means you better get your ass to church and do some repenting for you've broken some mighty calcified midwestern laws.

For example, consider the following phrases and their subtext: "Oh, for cute! Look at your ear muffs!" "Whowee! What a pretty lake you live on. It has an interesting sparkle." "You're having a barbecue on Thursday? For sure, we'll be there!" When you think the ear muffs really look like white, hairy asses; you know that the lake is really a secret dumping ground for old computers and televisions; and you already know you're never showing up at that barbecue. While friendliness is an issue of ethics, lying about your true opinion in the name of friendliness and agreeability is morally sound.

Apart from the morally sanctified fibbing to uphold appearances, what's actually problematic about this ubiquitous moral code of friendliness and agreeability is the apparent lack of discernment. Swindler or saint, garbage can or the dumpster man, a rabid hyena or the neighbor lady named Gina—no matter, all deserve equal treatment, a big smile, and your standard generosity, where considering the true motives of someone only points the finger back at yourself for the misdeed of even *thinking* such things about another soul.

And, less than a decade old, I already know—this wiggly line between truth and illusion makes me anxious. In a world of pleasantries, gossip, and compulsory warmth, what could I believe? Who and what can I trust?

These questions have itched at me for months.

Back in the bar, while my mother shakes her purse, listening for any clinking at the bottom of the bag, our father Tom and stepfather Bruce lean against the bar a few feet away from Donny and me. I'll be told later that my father, mother, and stepfather palling around together was unusual among divorced families, but my brother and I don't know any different. Bruce ordered a sausage pizza that now sits growing cold on the high-legged table in front of Donny and me. Donny will grow up to be a stocky, muscular man with eyes as green as my mother's. But at seven, he's a pudgy-faced cherub with a mop of brown curls. When the pizza arrived minutes ago, we each eagerly bit into a piece only to simultaneously scald the tops of our mouths before we spat out the mutilated pieces where they cooled, cheese spewed tentacle-like across the rest of the pizza. I run my tongue against the top of my mouth from front to back and feel the burned skin hang like a saggy awning while my father tells a story at the bar, about some hunting or fishing trip or some time up north. His hands fly wildly, his blue eyes widen and contract; he snorts, he guffaws, laughs manically, and takes a swig of his beer within the space of thirty seconds. Donny and I can't hear the story above the music but we can guess the plot and whether it's a tragedy, comedy, or farce from his theatrics. This time, he's talking about our ever-absent stepmother who's currently visiting her sisters in Alaska.

My father is a forty-five-year-old poster boy for Nordic facial features, with high cheekbones, a sturdy straight nose, and blond hair. He talks loud and wears a monstrous coyote fur coat during the winter to make up for his short stature. An entrepreneur who has sold caskets and run a vending machine business and peddled Rascal Scooters to nursing homes, he's currently between gigs.

Our father sets his beer down and settles onto a bar stool. His story over, Bruce lights another cigarette and chimes in with his own story. Bruce's still in his work clothes, a sweater and pressed shirt suitable for his job doing something I don't understand with numbers and diagrams and case files at an energy company. Bruce looks like a red-headed Steve Miller if he graduated from being a midnight toker to a business analyst with a Magnum P.I. mustache and comb-over. At forty, his face is still plump and childlike. If Bruce stood up straight, he'd tower over my father. But he doesn't. He avoids talking politics, laughs at my father's jokes, and keeps the peace.

My mother saunters up to Donny and me, her hooped earrings swinging back and forth, and plops a dollar in quarters that she got at the bar onto the greasy table and tells us to take some if we want to play pinball. She discards the mauled pizza Donny and I spat out, grabs a slice for herself, and winks at me. I shut my eyes, kick against the table to spin on my stool, and hope she'll be gone when I slow to a stop.

I am mortified to be in her presence.

Days earlier, I shoved a jumbled deck of black-and-white tarot cards in one of her old purses. I hoped the purse would chew their weird little black-and-white selves up and digest them into thin air. Gone and out of my life.

But today my mother found them just as I'd left them.

The day after we took our Christmas tree down, I'd taken my saved allowance and boarded the city bus to the local bookstore. As I watched the busy main streets go by, I looked in my pocket and counted my fortune. I had twenty dollars—I felt rich.

And I had a goal.

Once at my stop, I got off and wandered the half-mile to the bookstore, stomped the snow off my boots, swung the glass door open, and went straight to the "Spiritual" section—I wanted to find out the truth about This Place. I wanted to know what I could trust, what was real and true. I'd seen horoscope readings in the newspaper and thought that they could be my portal—with their pithy advice and location in the classified section, they seemed trustworthy.

The next logical step toward understanding seemed to be in this very bookstore.

I skimmed the selection and settled on three items: an Aries Sun Sign "Day-By-Day Horoscope Forecast Guide" for 1998; a used palm-reading book with a shiny, psychedelic cover and PALM READING written in fat, friendly letters; and the cheapest pack of tarot cards. Back at home, I sat on my bedroom floor and investigated. The astrology book forecast a daily prediction about my nonexistent love life and nonexistent career and other such adult concerns that didn't seem to apply to my winter break of sledding and macaroni-and-cheese dinners and building forts out of the stained couch cushions. In the palm-reading book, I read the "Mound of Venus" section and stared into my puffy pink hands, trying to discover my inner world through the grooves and pads of skin. I decided I needed more light. Standing by the window, I held my Mound of Venus in the sunlight, trying to determine how thick the lines that ran across my palm were. They all looked small. I gave up on palm reading and ripped the plastic off the tarot deck.

Placing the cards one by one in an arc across my floor, I watched the images unfold. A Devil, flying swords, strange scribblings, ominous-looking figures playing with disks . . . *These are supposed to help me understand my life?* This isn't what I thought my life was supposed to look like. According to my horoscope, I'm supposed to have passionate, robust lovers! A possible summer fling! Some potential family disputes, but a business opportunity that would give me the chance to put money away for my retirement!

I didn't like these cards. They were creepy and dark and confusing. I scooped them up, ran into my mother's closet, shoved them into a leopard print purse, and ran, yowling, out of the room.

For a few days, I forgot all about them.

Then this morning, my mother breezed into the living room while I was watching television and asked me what were these *things* she found in her closet? She held the cards out to me.

The tarot cards.

I threw myself on the rug and burst into tears.

"What . . . What's wrong?! What is *wrong*?" she asked.

I told her that I didn't know—I didn't know why the cards scared me. But they did. A lot.

My mother paused. I knew why she was suddenly upset— it's not because I ran into her room and shoved the cards in her purse. It's not because I bought them. It's because I'm inexplicably sobbing on the living room floor.

"Well, sheesh! They're just a bunch of cards! I just don't know why I ended up with them. But if they *scare* you that much, I'll just get rid of them," she said and stalked off to the adjoining kitchen. Still collapsed and sniffling on the floor, I heard the trash can opening, the rustle of a drop, the lid closing, and my mother sighing to Bruce, "I don't know what the problem is."

Goodbye, cards . . .

The idea that life could be filled with darkness, mystery, and suspicious disks was something I had never considered. Even if the cards were now carousing with raw egg and the spaghetti Donny dumped on the floor, their potential to reveal an unknown reality populated by Devils and death and sharp pointy objects still unnerved me.

Those cards . . .

Those cards could've told me anything. I had wanted to know the truth—but I hadn't considered that the truth could be just as anxiety-inducing as not knowing anything at all.

B ack in the bar, my mother watches as my spin stills to a stop. She's still there when I raise my head. She puts one hand on my shoulder and pushes back the blonde bangs that hide my eyes, holds my gaze, and asks if I'm doing okay.

I look her straight in the face, run my tongue across the burned skin in my mouth like I'm revving an engine, and flat-out lie to her.

"I'm good."

Bk tht's whl your Sapposed to do.

She pauses.

"Are you sure?"

"Umhmm." I nod.

"Okay . . ." She pulls away and watches Donny flipping levers on the pinball machine.

I know she doesn't believe me.

And I know that she knows I know.

Donny squeals as the silver pinball pings around the machine. He scores. The lights blink and flash. My mother goes to him, places her hand on his back, and as I breathe in the funk of two dozen cigarettes I wonder what would happen if I told her that I bought those cards because I just wanted to *know,* to understand This Place, to find guidance beyond our trite repartee and hushed hearsay. Would she believe me? Would she understand?

Later that night, after my mother has kissed my forehead and her feet have pattered down the hall, after Bruce starts to snore and Donny has stopped twisting and turning in his bed, I grab a tiny flashlight from my nightstand drawer and slink into the dark kitchen.

Standing on the tiled floor, I pause. Cabinet doors hang open around me. A chipped candy bowl sits barren. A single banana grows brown and soft on the countertop. My mother recently put up hideous maroon-and-white striped wallpaper that she started ripping off only a week after its debut. Strips reach outward like Spanish moss off a branch. I look at the garbage can sitting against the wall.

Those cards . . .

Those cards could tell me anything.

I *need* those cards, those pointy swords, those strange men doing things with disks. I had been too hasty in my dismissal of them. Maybe they could still help. Maybe I needed to trust that they could.

I walk to the garbage can, take the lid off, and look into the debris. The stench hits me—it's that earthy funk of moldy coffee grounds surely festering somewhere in this bag—but I am not deterred. I place the lid on the floor, hold the flashlight between my teeth, and plunge my fingers into the mess. I dig through spaghetti noodles and egg shells. Through coffee filters, receipts, and banana peels . . . I dig through all of it until I reach the cards and extract them one by one until I have the whole slimy deck before me on the kitchen floor.

I step back from the garbage can and run my hands underneath the faucet. Wiping them on my flannel pajamas, I turn back to the cards, wrap them in a dry dishrag, and tip-toe back upstairs to my room.

I place the cards underneath my bed, slide under the covers, and close my eyes. And as I drift into sleep, angst pulsing through me, I wonder if I could deal with a future that could hold both swords and cups, wands and pentacles, bliss and anguish.

Off Script

Your Reading For: December 21, 2000

Young Ram, you may have spent the past few years digging into all things celestial but you still must contend with life here and now. Remember— your soul chose This Place as its paradise. Now why might that be?

The only reason I'm here is because my mother said that if I came with her she would take me out to lunch and a movie afterwards. I am twelve and sit next to her in a pair of dark jeans and a calico sweater whose sleeves now resemble a wet cast from my own snot and tears. We're at the funeral of one of my mother's coworker's ninety-something father in a mildewy Methodist church south of town. I do not know the man whose picture beams in an ornate golden frame from the front of this chapel. I've never seen his oily white comb-over or his yellowed dentures or his tweed coat in person, but something—maybe the lyrics asking the Lord to abide by my side because the darkness has deepened or the contrast between all this black funeral garb and the cheeriness of the flowers at the front of church or maybe because this man, this ninety-something-year-old man who died just looks so content and unsuspecting of his mortality in that photo, I don't know—but something about the whole situation devastates me. From the moment my mother and I plop down in the wooden pews and examine our programs, I begin to blubber, heartache steadily rising in my body like raw yeasty dough until I spill all over the pew—mucus and tears, frantically wiping my nose against my sweater, squelching sobs, wanting to crawl under

> The truth = death will always arrive

Portent of what to come

19

the pew, or run out of the sanctuary and wail by myself in the ladies' room. Instead, I stay put and stifle myself. I pretend I'm sealing myself shut like a jar of canned pears locked away in a dank basement. I try to channel the lid clamping down, interlocking with the grooves of the glass jar. *Spin the lid 'round and 'round.*

In a black suit with a lilac scarf tied around her neck, my mother is either ignoring me or I've legitimately been quiet this far. *She could be a face on Mount Rushmore . . .* My serene matriarch, she exists on a different plane where turmoil doesn't touch her. Meanwhile, the jar image isn't working. The tears won't stop. My nose gushes. I try to calculate each breath to make sure I don't let a whimper escape, to suffocate this outpouring, to talk myself through the illogicalness of my unfounded mourning. *You don't know this man! You never knew him! Why are you crying?!*

Halfway through the service my mother readjusts her scarf to tuck the lilac ends into her blazer when she catches a glimpse of me balled up on the pew next to her with my eyes fixed to the floor, watching the interplay of lines and dots on the carpet's pattern move against my retinas in a psychedelic dance. I can hear her rummaging through her purse, my gaze still anchored away. She drops a handful of Kleenexes into my lap while whispering in my ear, "It's okay, Court. He was an old, old man."

I sit up, desperate for the tissues. "I can't help it—it's so— *sad.*"

My mother returns to watching the service and I wipe my nose as shame blossoms through me. My soaked sweater sleeves grow cold.

I've gone off script.

Later, after lunch, we sit in a dimly lit movie theater, the spongy seats creaking beneath our weight as advertisements for the local orthodontist and movie trivia flash on the screen. Popcorn crunches around us. The floor is sticky and scuffed. My mother hands me the bag of popcorn. I am heavy with humiliation; I feel as though I can barely lift my hand to grab it from her.

"Mom," I whisper. "I'm sorry I cried."

She pauses and pivots in her chair to look at me, her jaw hanging loose.

"Well . . . that's okay! That's okay you cried. You don't have to apologize—you just get so *upset* sometimes. I *worry* about you . . ." she says, popping a kernel into her mouth.

"Okay," I reply, relieved, and take the popcorn from her. I shove a handful into my mouth and listen to it crunch as the theater's lights go dark and the previews start.

In the years since I first encountered those tools of the Deep End—astrological readings and tarot cards and messages inscribed in my palm—I learned that my mother was a Pisces and I was an Aries. I learned about the different suits of Wands and Swords and Cups. I learned to find my heart and head line. I learned, despite my curiosities and repeated trips back to the bookstore, that I still didn't really understand the elusive *truth* about This Place that had led me to the bookstore in the first place. But maybe I already understood it—the theater of midwestern pleasantries was just that: a theater. But more than that, other questions are now more pressing.

The movie starts. Tom Hanks' face hovers onscreen—he's going to be stranded on an island. I'd seen the previews. Maybe what I really needed to find out was why my tears and tragedy at the funeral of a stranger? Why *do* I get so upset?

I look up at my mother intently watching the screen, her face illuminated by the film's glow. Why does my mother seem to exist on this plane where trauma doesn't touch her? Why is she my placid matriarch? How am I—weeping and emotive—her daughter? Is there any really any reason for her to fret?

I turn back toward the movie screen. *Maybe there is no reason . . .*

In the weeks and years that followed, while my friends were roller-blading on sidewalks and reading the dirty passages from *Flowers in the Attic* and smearing glitter on their faces and going to school dances, I charted the invisible forces of the solar system via astrology. I spent hours at the library looking up my mother's natal chart and my own, awash in a titillated stupor. There was something risqué and sexy about astrology—too shy to think about the sweaty bodies my friends were studying at school dances, thinking about the relationships between planetary bodies felt delicious and deviant.

Using the date, time, and location of one's birth, the natal chart reveals the energies that fuel a person during her or his lifetime. Modern astrologers describe the natal chart as an internal wiring that is neither inherently positive nor negative. It is a diagram of one's internal workings, like a computer hard drive or the backside of a calculator. Astrology is a metaphorical, often poetic, interpretation of the placement and relationships among planets, the twelve zodiac houses, and signs, which can detail one's gifts and challenges.

I peeled books off dusty library bookshelves and found used copies of astrological guides from the seventies at garage sales and dug through online archives. I looked up where Venus and Mars and Pluto were in our charts. I examined how the planets related to one another and how these relationships manifested in our behaviors. I explored the asteroids of Chiron, Ceres, and Juno. I read books about the right flower essences to ingest and which healing stones to put underneath our pillows based on the challenges outlined in our charts. I read past-life analyses and explored Vedic astrology, native to India. I read astrological interpretations that made our lives sound like soap operas and I read interpretations that were fatalistic and farcical. But I also read interpretations that revealed truths about myself and my mother that seemed to explain the whys and hows of our respective natures. Not only did astrology leave me euphoric but it also seemed to impart knowledge I couldn't find elsewhere.

My mother's chart showed a reserved woman with a fragile emotional world. It showed a woman who was cooperative, with an inclination toward working in the healing arts and with children and nature. It showed a social butterfly, a woman who attracted many friends and lovers, a woman who needed to respect her limits. My chart showed a girl with a strong inclination toward the occult. It showed a girl too serious for her age, a girl plagued by nervousness and anxiety, a girl with rapidly changing emotions. It showed a girl who was deeply attached—perhaps too attached—to her mother.

So, among other behaviors, me impulsively throwing those cards in my mother's closet? Me weeping at strangers' funerals? My mother's mellow composure and love for social events? It all made

Jumping off the Deep End !!

sense. The Deep End was a secret wormhole that led me straight toward wisdom. At teenage birthday parties, when I would inevitably cry at the sob stories of breakups and parents' divorces, and friends would turn to me with concern over my tears, I would say, "Don't worry—I'm fine. It's just my Moon. It's in Aquarius—my emotions are spontaneous." When Donny and I would grow older and were assigned to take our family's trash out and we'd gaze at the plethora of empty wine, beer, and hard liquor bottles in the recycling, I would say, "This is a part of how the universe works, Donny. Our mother *is* a Pisces. You know what they say about drinking and fish." When I would sit next to my mother at the local bars and watch her shove nickel after nickel into the slot machines and she would win again and again, I would think, *Yes, she is a lucky woman. It's the way Venus relates to Jupiter in her chart.* And at lunch, when friends would whine about their mothers— their possessive maternal ways and horrible rules—despite my inability to contribute to those conversations, I took solace in the fact that I could point to my sense of devotion to my mother—the sense of comfort and connection I felt to her over anyone else in my very natal chart. But despite these revelations, it was not until I was sixteen that I shared any of this with her.

I've run down the stairs to my bedroom to find my mother perched on the edge of my bed reading the astrology book I'd left open there this morning before I left. I'd spent the summer day lolling around my friend's grassy backyard looking through a waterlogged acupuncture guide I'd found at a thrift store. We sat on musty beach towels and tried it out, reading the diagrams and poking at our bodies. We squeezed our palms and fingers to stimulate our guts and giggled. We peeled our sneakers and socks off to push at our gummy feet, trying to reach serenity. We took turns holding one another's wrists to balance our livers. But eventually, our thumbs grew tired and our feet grew stinkier and we gave up as the sun sank lower in the sky and I unsuspectingly rode my bike home and clomped down to my room.

And as I see my mother sitting there reading that book all the harmony and peace I'd supposedly fostered in myself via the wonders of acupressure dries up to be replaced by nausea-inducing dread. My mother is reading this book about the Deep End. My mother knows I've gone off it. My mother knows my toes are pruning. Why did I leave that book there? Why did I mark her *name* on a Post-It Note and stick it in the corresponding chapter? Why is she reading it? And what is she thinking now that she's discovered it?

She studies the page as the late-afternoon sun streams through my bedroom's slatted shades, painting her in stripes. Mud cakes her fingernails. Stray grass blades stick to her legs. She's been planting mums and violets out in the yard. My arches tingle and I wonder if all that pushing on my feet has bruised them.

She holds a book about North and South Node astrology—an aspect of astrology that doesn't deal with physical bodies, like planets, but with the points between them. North and South Node astrology contemplates the Nodes of the Moon, the points formed by the Moon's orbit around the earth intersecting with the earth's path around the sun. From these points, each person has a South Node and a North Node. The South Node is the energy your soul carries with you into this lifetime, what you know how to do, what you understand, what you've already done. Your North Node is your soul's challenge for this lifetime, what is most psychologically difficult, what you are most unfamiliar with, what you must do in order to transcend self-defeating habits. It was the aspect of astrology that fascinated me most.

"Hi, Mom," I whisper still standing in the doorway, holding the acupressure guide close.

"Hi, Court," my mother says, her eyes fixed on the book.

". . . What are you up to?" I ask.

"Oh, just reading . . ."

"Oh."

"Courtney," she says, tilting her head to look at me. "Where did you find this?"

". . . The book?"

"Yeah."

"Uh, at the used bookstore on Madison Street."

She looks back at the pages, "This is . . ."

I brace myself.

Blasphemous? Disgraceful? Delusional?

"... me."

I run my fingers against the acupuncture guide's warped pages, uncertain of how to respond.

"This is *me*, Courtney." p. 22

"... What do you mean?"

"I mean, *this* part, this part ... It's weirdly me. I suppose that's why you put my name here. It's a ... I couldn't even say this about myself, but ... it's me."

She gapes at the cover.

"What *is* this exactly?" she asks.

"Well ..." I reply and explain it—you know, it's about astrology! North Nodes! South Nodes! Destiny! Challenges! Your soul! Your life's purpose and all—

She nods and flips through the pages, "Cool."

Cool?

Cool.

"Well ... that's great, Mom. I'm glad you like it."

Smirking, she looks at me and wiggles her eyebrows.

"Let's find your father's."

My father's?

Tentative, I shuttle over to her. We find the Nodes of his Moon via a chart in the front of the book and read aloud the mysteries of his past lives, soul, and life path. All the while my mother giggles— at his exhibitionist tendencies and lessons to be learned as a partner, chuckling at his naïveté and innocence, chortling at his need to be *needed.*

"Yes ..." she shuts the book closed. "That's him."

Outside my basement window, the sun has disappeared below the horizon, my mother's gardening tools left scattered throughout the lawn. I flip a lamp on.

"... I—I have more. More books and things ..." I say.

"Well, go get them," my mother replies.

"Okay ..." I reply, going to my closet and finding my astrology books. I emerge, toss them on to my unmade bed, and wait for her reaction. The covers are all esoteric wonder. They're all astrological glyphs and zodiac wheels and chakras radiating and auric bodies. My mystical fascinations revealed.

She looks at me.

I look at her.

Is this all too much? Is this where she will disown me? Will she now realize that I have now not innocuously just waded into the Deep End, but have fully immersed myself?

"... What are you thinking?" I whisper.

"Well, come here and show me what to do with them," she says, patting the bed next to her.

Maybe she already knew I was into all of this, this isn't a surprise. Maybe she didn't know and didn't care. Or maybe this isn't as risqué as I thought. I sat down next to her and we stayed up late into the evening reading about my father's astrological portrait. With each new element that I read aloud to her, she laughed. She shrieked hearing about his brashness and tendency to overspend as outlined by his Sun sign. She howled in glee at his impulsiveness and inclination toward outlandish attire as outlined by Venus. She was bowled over hearing about his sensitivity and fleeting generosity by the sign of Cancer in his chart. I kept reading to her and she kept laughing; belly heaving in and out, her shoulders shaking, tears streaming from her eyes.

"It's so true—it's funny," she kept saying, gasping.

I wasn't sure why it was so funny—maybe it was healing to hear about the personality flaws of her ex-husband that she had experienced firsthand. Maybe it was spite that caused her to roll in laughter on my bed that evening. Or maybe she was laughing at herself for marrying him nearly thirty years ago. Or maybe it really was so true it was funny. But no matter the reason, with that, my mother and I began to explore the Deep End together. To my elation, the person I felt most yoked to wanted to explore the subject I felt most compelled by.

That night, as I collected the books I had hauled out to put back in my closet, I stopped to skim through the highlighted sections of the North and South Node astrology book—I had marked the features of my mother's chart and my own.

My mother's North Node was in Sagittarius, ruled by Jupiter. Rather than flip-flop and placate to match the feelings of those around her, she must discern, believe in, and express her own personal truth. If the Nodes of the Moon could speak, they would say that my mother's goal was to transcend silence. My North Node was in Pisces, ruled by Neptune. Rather than obsessively worry about the future and find fault with everything that I encounter, my challenge was to accept the ebbs and flows of life, to trust the universe, and to believe, regardless of how it may appear, that everything is working toward a larger, more positive whole. According to the diagnosis of my Moon Nodes, my goal was to transcend doubt.

As I stood staring at the book, the thought of my mother transcending *silence* seemed strange. What was she silent about? How was she reticent? She was sociable and fun. She told me family secrets and rumors. She told me about her patients' ailments. And what did I doubt? Sure, I doubted the validity of such midwestern pleasantries and pondered its subtext, but this seemed to be more about *discernment*—not doubt. What was there to doubt? I had discovered the Deep End of mystical and prophetic wonders! I felt awash in answers! Enlightenment!

As I threw those books back into my closet and bounded upstairs to find a handful of saltines for dinner, I did not consider that what lies beyond the boundaries of such credulous faith is skepticism sprawling like the farmland around me, hills upon hills upon hills of lush, abundant uncertainty.

Sally's Chart

Your Reading For: June 24, 2007
    While it may be fun to investigate astrological
obscurities of asteroids and the like, remember
the center of your chart: the Sun. Remember her
message about patience. You cannot know everything at once, restless child.

Our guide to the Deep End was Linda Goodman. She
was our goddess, our bookshelf astrologer and
spiritual teacher whom we read and reread for the wisdom from
the universe. Her popular astrology books, released in the late 1960s
and '70s, illuminated the birth of the Age of Aquarius and the so-
called New Age. Her debut, *Sun Signs*, was the first book about
astrology to make it onto the *New York Times* Best Sellers list. For
many, Goodman lit a passage to discovering more about astrology
and all things mystical. Some even argue that Goodman spear-
headed the New Age movement in the United States through her
enormously popular astrology books. *Sun Signs* sold more than
five million copies. Her book *Love Signs* also made it onto the
New York Times Best Sellers list. Goodman was paid an unprece-
dented $2.3 million for the paperback rights.

Linda Goodman was born Mary Alice Kemery in 1925. Kemery
took the name "Linda" while hosting a radio show called *Love Letters from Linda* where she would read love letters from soldiers to
their spouses and lovers and vice versa accompanied by a romantic
song. After meeting her second husband, Sam O. Goodman, she
took his name and began writing speeches and newspaper articles.

According to her friends, Goodman always had an interest in
spirituality, but it was when she moved to New York in 1963 that

her interest in astrology flourished. Hunched over a coffee-table astrology book and charts, she spent up to twenty hours a day analyzing charts and writing *Sun Signs* in a bathrobe. After its publication, Goodman became, arguably, the most influential astrologer in the world, with her blend of keen insights and personable writing style.

When not writing about astrology, Goodman tried to prove the truth about two particular preoccupations. The first of these was proving the location of Osiris' phallus underneath the Hollywood Cross on Pilgrimage Drive in Cahuenga, California. Between 1970 and the early 1990s, Goodman spent a pint-sized fortune attempting to map the inside of the Hollywood Cross hill. She tried to rally interest and support for the project, and while surveys did suggest a structure was buried under the Cross, she died before she could prove it was the mystery member.

She spun many other conspiracy theories until her death in 1995, but Goodman's main concern after her search for Osiris' phallus was the death of her daughter Sally. Sally deliberately overdosed on Demerol and was found dead in her New York apartment in 1973. She was eighteen years old. A note, previous suicide attempts, and a positive identification by Goodman's second husband and Sally's stepfather closed the case. Cause of death was determined: suicide.

Goodman flew to New York and slept outside St. Patrick's Cathedral in Manhattan for ten days to draw attention to what she believed was an official cover-up of her daughter's fate. She claimed the evidence of her daughter's suicide was fabricated—the suicide note wasn't in her handwriting, the corpse's hair was bleached though Sally was a natural blonde, the corpse was too heavy, too tall. It wasn't her daughter. Goodman contacted the FBI and the CIA and claimed the government had staged the entire thing. She spent $400,000 on trying to find Sally and prove she was alive. Goodman used Sally's natal chart as her proof—she was convinced that Sally had been taken. Her chart indicated amnesia, seclusion, and being stowed away in a convent or by the government. Goodman's trust in the planets led her to believe in the seemingly impossible.

Twenty months earlier, Goodman's lover, Robert Brewer, had ventured to Mexico and was never seen again. She continued to set a place for him at her table for years afterward in the expectation that he would one day return to her. According to a friend, Sally's death plunged Goodman into the delusion that both Brewer and Sally could be found and, given her fortune, detectives and investigators took advantage of her by looking into cases that had already been proven. Goodman died a recluse at seventy in Cripple Creek, Colorado, having never reunited with Sally or Robert and with Osiris' supposed phallus still buried and waiting to be discovered beneath the Hollywood Cross.

During my teenage years, I was enthralled with Goodman—her story, her writing, her thoughts on astrology, our shared Sun sign, Aries. But I didn't understand Goodman's obstinacy with regard to her daughter's death. Why did she not accept that her daughter had died? Why did she continue to live in a delusion that her lover would return? Was it a delusion? Despite her love for him, shouldn't Goodman, of all people, have known the truth about his whereabouts? Despite her feelings about the inconsistencies of Sally's corpse, were there other signs that pointed to her suicide that she ignored? What were the signs around Linda Goodman, if any?

I didn't know—like most of her fascinations, the answers to my questions, too, were a mystery.

Meanwhile, I had also become enthralled with the idea of messages from the universe revealed in coincidences or synchronicities. As a self-absorbed Aries, I loved the idea of the universe speaking personally to me. I had begun taking everything potentially to mean something: the way toothpaste squeezes onto a toothbrush, the number of stripes on a red-and-white candy peppermint, the serial number on a parking ticket—all could be endowed with the secrets of the universe and should be pondered with great consideration concerning their strategic appearance in my life.

I'd call friends with prophetic happenings: "I heard *three* James Taylor songs on the radio today and then the clerk at the gas station's name was 'J.T.' This must *mean* something." Or "I had a dream about ten men dressed up in pantyhose and, in the dream, we drank champagne. And then today champagne was *on sale* at the store! This must mean something. Is this is a sign that I should research things about France? Does this mean I was French in another life? Or . . . do you think the champagne could be *contaminated* with strange fibers and that's why it's on sale?"

My friends would respond with something like, "Courtney. I think you just—I think you need to stop calling me with this stuff. If the 'universe' or whatever wants you to know something, you'll know. You won't have to wonder."

When I actually had a prophetic dream at seventeen, I called Donny from a scuzzy payphone outside a gas station to share the good news. When he picked up, I began telling him of my good fortune.

"*Donny.* Guess what? I had a prophetic dream! Last night, I dreamt that Dad's car would die in the street today *and it did*! He let me borrow it and I was driving and it died and now it's in the middle of State Street and I'm looking at it right now and I saw it last night. Isn't that amazing? The universe is amazing!"

"Wait—what? Dad's car died?" he sputters.

"Yes! AND I ALMOST PREDICTED IT."

"But, Court, his car *died* . . . I, I think you need a tow truck, right?"

My mother, however, was most fascinated by the afterlife. *What happened? Where do you go? Could you speak to your loved ones?* After her parents, Della and Albert, died, my mother believed their souls had temporarily incarnated into the two cardinals that inhabited our backyard. She would watch the cardinals with binoculars from the deck and yell to whoever was listening inside the house, "Albert is on the windowsill!" Some mornings she would shake me awake, telling me to come and say hello to my grandparents before they flew away. Sometimes I would go to the window to see my grandparents fidgeting on a branch. Sometimes I would watch as they propelled themselves into flight. And sometimes I would run to the window to find bare tree limbs trembling in the wind.

But today we've already seen the cardinals come and go. We're already gone swimming in the lake and taken a walk through the woods and found a mouse skull in the grass. We've already made a pot of coffee and drank it while watching a rerun of *Beaches* on television and prank-called Donny to whom we moaned about our boredom pretending to be his estranged aunts from Finland. After Donny figures out it's us and hangs up, telling us we're *too old* for this kind of shit—I'm nineteen and home from college from the summer, my mother is fifty-two and has the day off from work—my mother decides that we should take a drive.

"Where to?" I ask.

"Let's go to Della and Albert's," she suggests.

"They don't live there anymore. It's not like they're gonna invite us in for a cocktail or something," I reply.

"I *know* they don't live there anymore. Let's just take a drive to see it—I haven't been there in years."

So we pile into the car, roll the windows down, and drive west past the dairy farms and mud-caked trucks putzing along the highway. We drive until it's all blotchy grass, dirt roads, and abandoned cars rusting in gravel driveways. We drive until the pale green house on the left appears and my mother turns the engine off.

We step out of the car, slam the doors shut, and stand, staring at the house. It's humid; we're both glistening, still wearing our bathing suits and shorts. I'd been to their house before when I was a little girl, but I didn't remember it looking this way. Someone bought the house after Della and Albert died, but it looks abandoned: The roof warped. Paint chipping. The sidewalk up to the porch nearly rubble; unkempt grass sprawls on either side of the walkway. A dog howls behind a chain-link fence down the road, his voice distant and mournful.

I look at my mother as she stares at the house, her face soft and melancholic as though she were adrift in memory. I slap a mosquito off my thigh.

"Did I ever tell you that Della thought she was intuitive, like, you know, a psychic?" my mother whispers.

"No . . . I don't think so."

She slouches against the car.

"Yes, she predicted the neighbors' death back in the sixties."

I turn to face her.

She continues, whispering about how Della supposedly foresaw that the neighbor was going to kill his wife and stage it as an accident or suicide. Then the wife was found with a men's tie around her neck. The coroner called it a suicide and no further investigation was done. But the neighborhood was in a speculative uproar.

Who could kill themselves with a tie? Was that even possible? After that, Della also foresaw that the husband would die. She wasn't sure how—but she felt it was going to happen.

Weeks later, a group of young men followed him home from a bar a few miles away with the intention of robbing him. They beat him to death in his kitchen.

"... Do you think she *predicted* it? Or did she just guess?" I ask.

"I don't know ... I was just a little girl. I just remember she *knew*," my mother replies.

We both turn to look at the house.

"My room was up in that attic," she says, nodding her head upward toward the roof.

"After that happened with the neighbors, I would just stay up all night wondering about their ghosts. You know, if they were still here. Maybe they were mad at Della—if she knew, then maybe she should've told the woman to leave. Sometimes ... the curtains would twist and I would wonder if it was them—the husband and wife, if they were arguing. The lights would flicker on and off ..."

"... Flicker?" I ask.

"Flicker."

"But. Wait. Mom. What—what do you mean the curtains would *twist*?" I ask.

"I mean, they would *move* and throw themselves around while I was lying in bed!"

"Were the windows open?"

"No!"

"Are you messing with me? Is this a joke? Did you drive me out here to tell me all these creepy things?"

"No! No! This all happened—the man, the woman, Della's predictions. The curtains! I was in that room!" She points to the window.

"Well. ... That's all really creepy, Mom."

"Yes," she says, her eyes widening. "It is."

I look up at the tiny attic window.

We shouldn't even be here—maybe we should've taken some sage with us. We should've brought crystals to bury in the ground here. We should say a prayer or hold a se—

A stray cat runs in front of the house and freezes at our presence.

None of us move. The cat keeps still, blinking in mid-trot.

I lean down and talk to it, "Hey kitty! Come here!"

Scrawny and gray, the cat adjusts her stance and glares at me. Her tail swipes to the left, to the right.

My mother chimes in cooing, "Come here, sweet kitty!"

It hisses at us, nostrils flared, and bounds into the overgrown boxwoods next door.

We crack up and get back in the car.

As we drive home, I wonder if I were to see a sign or message like my grandmother had supposedly intuited—something dire and horrifying—if I would be too scared to believe it. With my mother's left arm perched on the open driver's side window, she turns up the radio to sing along to Carly Simon. A sunburn rising on the tip of her nose, the word *maybe* breezes through me.

Five Years

Your Reading For: August 15, 2007
Impetuous little Ram! What nightmares will this forthcoming adventure inspire for you? Remember you are the compass and discernment is your tool.

Picture this: You want a drink, but not just any drink. You've no need for water or juice or diet soda. You want something that has to be opened by banging the cap on the side of a countertop. You want a beverage that will light up in your hand like a glow stick as the neon beer signs reverberate into your beverage. You want to drink this drink in a place replete with west-central Wisconsin tavern history, a history of vodka-induced brawls, of bats flying out from a back room and floating straight through the bar and inciting mass hysteria on one July night, a history that includes an annual fundraiser for a parakeet's medical bills and the local animal shelter, a history of cigarettes still being smoked even though that smoking ban in all public areas came into effect months ago, a history of the same locals sitting in the same spot in the same baseball caps at the same time drinking the same drink on their chosen day of the week. You want to drink your special drink in an environment of near pseudo-danger—where the locals see their spot at the bar as precious real estate. It's their turf, their boozy home that they've bought with dollars paid and hours spent. And, somehow, this tantalizes you—to walk into a bar and have everyone turn to look and see who is showing up at four in the afternoon on a Wednesday because everyone who's supposed to be here at four in the afternoon on a Wednesday is already here. So, they all ask with their collective stares, *Who are you to show up now?*

If you want that drink, take the country road three miles east from our house, take a right at the fork, pull into the first plot of dirt on the right, walk into Randy and Tammy's Bar, and take your seat at one of the orange Formica tables.

On a Wednesday afternoon later that same summer in August my mother wants such a drink. A drink *just like that*. And on a soon-to-be-failed raw-foods-only kick, obsessed by the vibratory energies of raw foods mingling with my soul and lifting me to some embodied spiritual ascension, I go with her and take a bag of carrots with me.

We walk into the dim, wood-paneled bar and find an open table. Signs advertising Bud Light and Zima and Coors glow along the back wall. It stinks like cigarettes and stale popcorn. The floor sticks to my sandals as I walk, the soles peeling away with my step as the regulars turn to glare at the two women who've wandered in here.

My mother grabs a beer. We sit down and I shove a carrot into my mouth as she begins to dig for change in her purse to play the slots when one of the regulars meanders over to see who showed up at four on a Wednesday. He's maybe sixty—a flannel-wearing, balding, bespectacled man sipping a Bloody Mary. My mother will talk to anyone so she pulls out the third chair at our table for him to sit in and keeps digging around in her purse.

"Well, hello ladies," he says, handing me a ring made out of a dollar bill. "I keep these for the young things." He puts it in my palm, his fingers stubby.

"Thanks," I say, shoving a carrot in my mouth to let my mother carry the conversation. After some cursory introductory information, he tells us he's clairvoyant.

Clairvoyant?

I perk up. *We found someone prophetic in this bar?!* I want to know everything—husbands, divorces, what color underwear would be most beneficial for me to wear next Saturday, etc. My mother takes a sip of her beer and listens as he prattles on about his great intuition and his past successful predictions. Swirling his nearly empty Bloody Mary around, he tells us his *feelings* about us.

Feelings?

"You need to be careful," he says to my mother. "I hate to tell you, I've never gotten this before, but I'm really getting the feeling that your death is imminent. Are you wearing your seatbelt? Taking all your vitamins? Getting yearly check-ups?"

My body grows stiff with tension. Her death is imminent?

My mother sips her beer. She shrugs, her face placid.

He continues, shaking his head.

"The phrase 'five years' keeps coming up in my mind. Five years left? Five years ago something happened? Five years . . ."

He then turns to me and I nearly jump out of my seat. "*You* need to be careful too! Careful about your choices. About what you're doing. Late at night. With others. You could get knocked-up within a year if you keep up with what you're up to. You young things, heh . . . is that what you want?"

He tells us more and I feel like I might twist into bits and disintegrate right at this table. He tells us about Bruce and Donny. About the world. About what's going to happen in This Place. About what might happen to this bar. *You know they had bats in here once . . .* It occurs to me that he might be poking fun at psychics. Maybe he woke up this morning and thought, *I'm going to go to Randy and Tammy's and tell some random people that I can predict the future and make up some shit. Watch 'em freak.* Maybe we were his joke. Women he could scare. Women he would laugh about later. I touch my mother's elbow and tap it. She taps her foot against mine, a secret code. As he talks about the farmer's future crops and how you can never believe what that Almanac says, I place the dollar-bill ring on the table and nudge it back toward him.

He finishes his monologue by reiterating that my mother needs to wear her seatbelt. *That's* what's really important, he says.

My mother looks at me, winks, and bursts out laughing. The man chuckles, seemingly relieved to be alleviated from our speechlessness. My mother finishes her beer in one gulp and suggests that we need to get back home. I bolt to the bathroom while she finishes the pleasantries, *Nice to meet you, thanks for sharing, gotta go—need to water the plants . . .*

I stare into the grimy restroom mirror, frantic and shaken. How old would my mother be in five years? How many ways could a fifty-seven-year-old woman die? Did something happen five years ago that we should be aware of? And for me, what does his forecast even *mean*? What is he talking about? I don't go out at night and canoodle with random people. There's no one to canoodle with in this dinky town! And my mother—my mother is *fine*. Everything is *fine*. I run my hands under the sink, splash water on my face, and look back at myself in the mirror.

The water doesn't help. Panic thrums through me. I forgot the carrots back at the table. I rush from the bathroom and into the gravel parking lot.

My mother is waiting for me outside and we beeline to the car. I get in the driver's seat and hitch my leg up on the side of the door while my mother slides in the passenger's seat. I look at her. She looks back. Her subtext, *What are you waiting for?*

"Well, you put your seatbelt on. Remember what the dude said."

"Well, you keep your legs together. *Remember what the dude said.*"

W̲e went home.

Now, you would *think* that, me being such a sucker for anything having to do with people claiming to be intuitive in any fashion, despite his dire predictions I would've hired this man to map my future and plan my outfits in accordance with Venus' cycles, but I wasn't sleeping around and refused even to consider my mother dying so young. For once, I told myself everything that my skeptical friends had said to me before about my mystical interests. These little coincidences you latch onto are nothing but randomness. You're creating self-fulfilling prophecies for yourself. Knowledge from the planets and the stars is total hogwash. All this spirituality that has to do with so-called inner-knowing is nothing but an excuse for narcissism and self-indulgence. What you call "wisdom" is backwards quackery. And on that drive home, I, too, assumed the entire experience to be bogus: counterfeit mysticism.

But here's the thing with astrology, the Age of Aquarius, and all that: What's really the point of it unless you actually know when you're having a meaningful, synchronistic moment? How much can we really know about the workings of the universe? Even with warnings or premonitions, will what is "fated" happen regardless of whether or not you know it? Is anything really "fated"? And, despite such emphasis on inner-knowing, how do you know when you're just being fed another midwestern euphemism or drunken fiction?

The Lake

Your Reading For: December 25, 2011
Yes, young Aries, you truly are the baby of the Zodiac with your innocent foibles and impulsive ways, but this does not mean that you cannot care for those who need your help.

My stepfather Bruce must've been a good boy this year. Instead of sitting in some cousin's duplex with all of our relatives smashed together on two sink-hole couches Christmas day, squinting through the cigarette smoke, escaping to the kitchen to dig around in the infamous bowl of Brandy Slush (heavy on the brandy, light on the slush) with a plastic ladle, everyone reveling in their debauchery yet making up for it by being dressed up in their Sunday best as we watch one of the cousins puke by the mailbox, Bruce gets to drive across the state to Lambeau Field, freeze, and watch the Packers play the Bears while my mother and I go to the annual family Christmas celebration by ourselves. Donny made the best choice, being off in Oklahoma playing club hockey and making a frozen pizza by himself.

Once at the soirée, we sit around and play cards as the colored Christmas tree lights strung around the perimeter of the living room glow. Tinsel drapes the fake tree in the corner and whenever anybody walks past it a few strands of tinsel attach themselves via static and follow them like their own personal streamers. By midafternoon, there's tinsel everywhere. Tinsel sprawled across the worn taupe carpeting. Tinsel attached to the plaster wall. Tinsel on the bathroom floor. Tinsel in our hair.

Meanwhile, my mother has consumed five glasses of wine, three beers, half of a mixed drink before I dumped it out, and a handful of wasabi-flavored almonds that I forced her to eat. Before everyone starts to leave and siphon off to their respective homes, someone demands that we take a family photo. *Gather by the fire! Get the little kids in front. Make sure your face can be seen! Hold up your drink! Smile! Say cheese!* I stand next to my mother on the end of the middle row and give her arm a squeeze.

She grins at me.

I grin back.

We face forward and wait for our cue.

Cheese!

My mother lifts her shirt up as the photo snaps.

Her elbow clonks me in the head and I turn to look at her—a bosom-filled violet lace bra with a strap slinking down one shoulder, brown leather belt around her waist holding up her slacks, a thin fleshy bulge protruding over the belt, belly-button dark and cavernous, the tanned outline of her halter-top bathing suit from last summer still visible on her chest, arms held to her collarbone like an easel displaying a masterpiece. *My presentation for you, dear family!*

"Mom—" I hiss.

She shrieks and giggles. This thrills her. Still holding the sweater, she shimmies. Our in-law holding the camera fumes in a nearly purple blush. The taller cousins in the back start to laugh. My mother's sisters are staring at us. The parakeet is staring at us. Everyone is staring at us. The two shih tzus sequestered in a bedroom start to bark. I pull her arms down and smooth her sweater over her stomach.

Good Lord.

Is this why Bruce was delighted at the opportunity to shiver on a metal bench halfway to Michigan? At least the Packers are probably winning.

I guide her arms down and wonder where my car keys are.

I drive her home.

She stumbles inside the house, drops the porcelain casserole dish we brought with us on the floor where it bounces and shatters like hail on pavement, puts *The Best of the Doors* on the CD player, blasts it, and dances across the kitchen with her winter coat half-on, half-off as I take my jacket off. She lets her purse fall from her grip and onto the floor with a thud. She stops and changes the track from "Hello, I Love You" to "Touch Me" and lets her coat fall. From the living room, the three-foot-tall papier-mâché elephant she bought last fall to go with her new tropical décor seems to watch her with his trunk raised in suspicion, *Stay away!*

I go into the kitchen closet to grab a broom to clean up the broken dish as she grabs me, pulling me to her and pressing her cheek against mine. She is all perfume and boozy breath and winter cold and she holds me like a teenage boy holds his pubescent sweetheart at the semi-formal, her arms around my waist, cozied close. She mumbles along to Jim Morrison, her body swaying against mine—

"Courtney!" she cries. "This is my favorite! I love this song!" She sings along louder as I slide my arms around her neck, dancing with her in a lumbering slow-dance.

"Now, Courtney . . ." she whispers. "Listen very closely . . ."

"I'm listening," I tell her.

She presses her mouth to my ear. I can see the broken dish and forgotten purse out of the corner of my eye as she tells me about the eternal nature of the soul. She tells me about how we never *really* die, about never being abandoned, about how we're here on earth to gain understanding, to learn how to forgive, and to recognize ourselves in others. And, most importantly, my daughter, we're here to *love*. I'm nearly tipsy myself as she whispers her own brand of esoteric wisdom to me. I close my eyes, buzzed on this spiritual serenade, totally go—

She throws her head back and shrieks.

"We need to Love. Just like the song says!" She spins away from me, stumbles into an ottoman, and plays riffs on an invisible drum kit. I grab the broom and watch her onstage at her own imaginary concert.

I roll with it. I'm the girl in the third row.

She holds her arms out to me and wiggles her fingertips, signaling me. I take the broom with me and walk toward her as she wraps her arms around me and the broom.

She presses her face to my ear again and whispers, "Courtney. When I die. I want you to throw my ashes into the lake. Put me there. In the water."

Put you in the lake?

I picture it—me spreading her ashes in that algae-ridden lake. That's where she wants to go? With the walleye and leeches and stringy seaweed? That's what she wants as her final resting place? It's hilarious. It's ridiculous. It's *weird*. I start to howl in laughter.

She sits back and scowls at me, throwing her hands into her lap, "I mean it, Courtney Ann. You're gonna put me in that lake . . ."

I fall silent.

"Okay. I'll do it. I'll put you in the lake . . ."

She grins and threads her arms around me again as "The End" bleats behind us in the background. I close my eyes, disappear into the scent of her familiar perfume, and feel myself grow slack in her embrace. The word *sign* does not float through my mind as I lead my mother to her bedroom. The word *prophecy* does not resonate within me as I sweep up the broken dish. As I slink downstairs to my room, I leave the remnants of the evening—the tinsel stuck to our pants, the abandoned coat on the floor, my mother speaking of her own departure—to slip away into my memory unexamined.

Small Town Girls

Your Reading For: July 23, 2012
     This isn't how it works, baby Ram—you can't just ignore advice if you don't like what it reveals. If you want to speak the language of the universe, you must take it in all forms—good or bad.

Five summers after we met the psychic man at the bar, I am twenty-four and my father's battered and worn workbench, white leather La-Z-Boy armchair, and collection of taxidermy mallards, wood ducks, and various other waterfowl, among other hastily duct-taped boxes and camouflage bags, appear in our garage one Monday. My mother and I arrive home from work—her from the hospital, me from the hotel—within minutes of each other to find my father's abandoned belongings. Bewildered by this cryptic collection, horrible fantasies about my father's demise surface. *He's being framed! He could've been robbed! He might be under threat! Why else would his stuff show up here?*

My mother stares at the pile and laughs.

"I know what happened," she says.

"What happened to him?"

"It's Virginia."

Virginia is my father's third and current wife.

"She—killed him?" I whisper.

She snaps her head, glaring at me.

"No, you goof. Virginia *ousted* him. She kicked him out."

My mother is right.

I call my father later to confirm my mother's suspicion that, yes, Virginia told him to leave their house and he dumped some

44

of his stuff in our garage. Or, in his story, he *decided* to leave and has taken up temporary residence at his sister's cabin down the road from my mother's house until he can find a more permanent landing place. My father and Virginia were talking divorce, who was getting what, what pieces of furniture were going to burn before the other one got to it. They were talking numbers and arguing over end tables and their three Labradors' water bowls and writing angry misspelled e-mails to each other, simultaneously proclaiming their absolute, undying love and their total, unadulterated hatred of the other.

When I report back the news to my mother, she replies with a Zen utterance: "They're going to be fine—this is what your father does." That afternoon she and I go shopping together. She picks out a bottle of red wine and a box of garlic-flavored crackers for him. As we check out, she tells me that he needs someone to talk to and I'm the only—no, the *best*—one to do it. She instructs me to open the wine and eat the crackers—he probably already has the cheese. Make sure he knows how to use the air conditioner and tell him he should put screens on the windows if they aren't already there.

She drops me off at the cabin. As she pulls away, she holds her hand out the window, fingers outstretched like a catcher's glove, and disappears into the distance.

I walk up to the cabin and pause to watch the siding's peeling paint twitch in the wind before opening the flimsy screen door to find my father with his own bottle of wine listening to the radio. Static snaps. Cross-stitched scripture and taxidermy bass line the cabin's dull avocado interior; a hologram Brett Favre clock gleams on the wall. My father raises his head to look at me. A whimper escapes from my mouth at the sight of him. His cheeks are wet and flushed with liquor. At fifty-nine, his face is weathered with deep smile lines and decades of sun, though there isn't a trace of gray in his blonde hair. I go and sit down next to him.

He brings out a block of cheese, we eat the crackers, and I listen to his diatribe against Virginia: everything that's awful, possibly scandalous, and detestable about her; her problems with money; turning all his white shirts pink when she does the laundry; and her jealousy over his two ex-wives. How she bakes lamb at the wrong temperature and should season salmon with dill and how that woman just needs more *friends*. He opens another bottle of wine. He tells me that he's done, he's over it. He gets up and slides a CD of Journey's *Greatest Hits* into the boom box. As he moves, he gives me advice, telling me to learn from his mistakes. These are the Secrets of Life! This is what fathers are for. This is what *times like this* are for! Learnin'! Livin'! He holds up the wine. Boozin'!

He looks at me with total earnestness.

"This—"

He points to the boom box, "This is *love*."

Press Play.

Song by song we listen to the entire *Greatest Hits* album as he explains the intrinsic meaning of each line by repeating the song lyrics with added emphasis and contributing his own occasional commentary. Being able to hang his inner world on the lyrics of eighties pop stars with long hair and tight jeans and testosterone wafting from their bodies who sang about love, longing, and heartache is his free pass to be sentimental. *I wonder if my parents really were meant for one another. They both like to impart life advice to their daughter via Greatest Hits albums . . .*

The synthesizer moans and Steve Perry sounds like some celestial 1980s god and my father warbles along before breaking into advice—about taxes, about what he should've done when he was my age, about that car trip he should've never taken—that's when he and Kenny Wineman got in that accident. "Don't Stop Believin'" plays and my father tells me he thinks the whole thing is a crock of shit—you know, maybe there are sometimes when you *shouldn't* believe, right? Right? My father chants along to "Wheel In the Sky" before telling me about what kind of car accessories never to buy—about when and why they're going to swindle me at the mechanic. The melodramatic rhythm of "Separate Ways (Worlds Apart)" throbs through the tiny cabin and he pounds his fists along to it and I am relieved for the slow lull of ballads where my father simply gazes, his eyes fixed beyond me, and mutters along to the lyrics until the album repeats.

Part Two of my initiation to The Secrets of Life begins with him telling me why his three marriages have "failed," beginning with his marriage to Virginia and going back chronologically to his first marriage, to my mother. He tells me about his life with her, about the trip to Mexico that ended in selling his watch to get enough money for both of them to catch a bus across the border, how my mother would measure out a tablespoon of butter to smear her toast each morning, about her fondness for taking in stray cats who would inevitably vomit tapeworms on their bed. He pauses. "You know, if, say, tomorrow, someone told me your mother had died, I wouldn't cry."

Leaning back in my chair, I cross my arms and feel myself stiffen.

"You wouldn't cry?" I ask.

"Nope. Why would I care? Why would I cry?"

"Because . . . you were married for over a decade and you have two children together and . . . you loved her?" I reply.

He thinks.

"I wouldn't cry. In fact, I wouldn't shed. A. Tear."

He takes another swig of wine.

I shove a cracker in my mouth.

I listen to it crunch and turn my head to watch moths gather on the porch light.

I look back at him.

He peels the label off a wine bottle. The paper rips.

I swallow and stare at the Brett Favre hologram behind him, the phrase *Why would I care?* clanging around my chest.

Signs

Your Reading For: August 20, 2012

Ah yes! We knew we'd come to this eventually! Remember, young Aries, that the traveler would be nowhere without the gentle teachings and grace of her homeland.

It was the dress code that clinched the job offer for me: *anything.* They said, *Almost anything you want. At György Vörösmarty Gimnazium, most teachers wear sneakers and t-shirts. It is very casual—very good for our American teachers who come.* The thought of not wearing a uniform excited me. I imagined turning in my hotel uniform, handing it clean and pressed over the front desk, giving them my name tag, waving goodbye, and frolicking through the parking lot. I imagined ripping the polyester uniform apart at the seams and tossing it into the air like confetti. I imagined my cry of glee.

It was also the location: *Just outside Budapest's city center. A short bus ride to galleries, parks, and cafés.* I remembered the images I'd seen of Budapest's Hero's Square: an ornate, marble-floored monument to honor seven Hungarian leaders flanked by two art galleries on either side with a zoo and a lush park beyond. I imagined bitter espresso hitting my tongue. I imagined steam rising off the Széchenyi baths with supposedly healing waters. I imagined visiting a mountain that I'd heard was an energy vortex in the Hungarian countryside.

It was the timing: *Immediately. Classes start in late August. Come a few days early for an introduction.* I saw myself kissing my mother goodbye, the twenty-four-year-old boomerang child tossing herself out into the world again, begrudgingly wriggling away from her orbit. I saw myself standing in the driveway, my bags packed, distraught to leave, telling myself that it's better to be homesick than to be home. And my mother standing opposite me, telling me I should leave This Place. That I'm young, I should do this. That I'll love it once I'm there. It's just the leaving that's hard. I saw her reminding me that she'd see me soon—in April, she'd come to visit. We'd go to the beach. We'd take a train straight to the Adriatic Sea. She'd buy a new swimsuit. *And I'll have to find matching sandals* . . . She'd wiggle her eyebrows, wrap her arms around me, and I would fantasize about staying there forever.

I take the job.

Just outside the city center" actually means a suburb forty-five minutes from downtown Budapest taking the metro system. It means a wasteland of sprawling strip malls, train tracks, and apartment complexes. "Just outside the city center" actually means a perfect area to study the foraging habits of pigeons, candy bar brands most commonly consumed and littered by high school students, and the facial expressions of bewildered tourists who have taken the tram much too far. "Just outside the city center" is not what I tell my mother about when she asks about Budapest— I tell her about the espresso, delicate bow-fashioned pastries, and salami. I tell her about seventeenth-century artwork and rhinos at the zoo and the parade downtown. I tell her about blue skies and art nouveau architecture. I give her a postcard and write euphemisms on the back.

Just outside the city center, the view from my apartment window looks across an indoor tennis court that has a curved white top. At night it resembles a bloated, glowing, drum-tight beached whale that has mysteriously made it all the way past Bosnia-Herzegovina, Croatia, and a chunk of Serbia to die in this Budapest suburb. I suspect my apartment, arranged by my employer, also serves as a storage unit. They have provided me with three twin-sized beds, four couches, two love seats, numerous chairs, two desks, two wardrobes, and five comforter sets along with assorted cookware. All of this was evenly dispersed like a furniture showroom when I arrived.

During my first week in Budapest, each evening when I would return from school and open the door to my studio apartment I would wonder if this collection was a sign. Does it mean they didn't intend for this space to be an apartment? Does it mean I'm not welcome? Does it mean that, metaphorically, I have become too cluttered and need a cleanse?

In actuality, it means I carve a nook for myself by the window and shove three of the couches, two beds, both love seats, all but one of the chairs, and one desk against one wall, pile the blankets and pillows I didn't need on top, put the wardrobes on the edge of the kitchen area, and throw a few sheets over the furniture collection. It means I never invite guests over. It means that when I'm not teaching fourteen-year-olds how to buzz the English "vvv" or pronounce *misanthrope*, I take that forty-five-minute journey to the city center, to the Budapest pictured in travel guides.

In my usual jaunts to the city center, I've met another spiritual enthusiast and fellow midwesterner, Tiffany, and we quickly become friends. Though we grew up just across the Minnesota-Wisconsin border from one another, we'd never met before. Seven years my senior, Tiffany trusts in tarot readings, knows her Sun sign and Moon sign, monitors Mercury's retrogrades, giddily looks at jaspers and quartzes with me, and is convinced that she was Hungarian in a past life. That was why she decided to spend a year abroad in Budapest. Like my mother, Tiffany is interested in the afterlife. Her mother died when she was twenty-seven and she carries many of the same questions as my mother: *What happens when you die? Where does your soul go? How does time progress for a soul? Can you communicate with those you left behind?*

Tiffany is beautiful in that midwestern way where beauty is a formula studied and learned from the women who have come before you. Her equation: *curlers + lashes + eating salads + the right bra + stair machine + concealer + something shiny on your neck or fingers or ears (fake or real) = glamour.* I would watch strangers watch her in bars and cafés. She got the answer right every time.

When I tell Tiffany about Dobogókő, a mountain of mystical vibrations and a history of bestowing spiritual visions upon visitors, a place said to be the location of the earth's heart chakra, she instantly agrees to come along. We want all that—the vibes, the visions, to feel our souls illuminated like never before.

In preparation for our journey, Tiffany and I promise one another to eat only vegetables for two weeks in advance. We buy sage and vow to smudge our bodies daily. We hide coffee grounds and bottles of vodka and red wine in the distant caverns of her neighbor's apartment and speak of our souls as bursting stars of love and light and peace. To bed at nine and to wake at four! No listening to disco and no stopping for sweets from the bakery and no ogling people on the metro. And even if neither of us ever go to bed at nine or get up at four and even if it's hard *not* to stare at people on the train, because what else do you have to *do* but stare, and even if we actually decide to loll in the bar drinking cappuccinos and eating pork rinds at noon before boarding the bus, we still keep saying to the other, in between wiping oily fingers on our jeans and running our thumbs along the rim of our coffee to catch any stray sugar, that *we gotta be pure for this.*

Our plan is to spend the day at the mountain, letting its high vibrations seep into our souls and shake up everything that had calcified and collected rust in our auras, and then visit a bath back in Budapest where we'd let the mineral waters wash our energetic bodies clean.

We arrive at the mountain and tromp onto a flat plane of prairie grass overlooking a wide valley. Oak trees in their full autumnal glory shiver around us. A group of German tourists with walking sticks meander past Tiffany and me. A little girl spins and blows bubbles with her gum while her parents consult a map. Men on motorcycles pull up beside the motor coach and light cigarettes, sauntering up to one another to smoke and chat. There aren't Tibetan peace flags. There isn't some mystical Technicolor sludge foaming beneath the grass. This isn't a lush vortex of vegetation as I had imagined the heart chakra of the earth to be. I was expecting orbs. I was expecting visions to hit me as I stepped off the bus. I was expecting visible auras to radiate from the trees.

"This is it!" Tiffany says, grinning, bounding ahead of me.

This is it?

We drift along the wooded trail and down the hill in silence, passing monuments, small chapels, and statues to commemorate spiritual visions seen on the mountain in centuries past. Despite my supernatural expectations, the trail is quaint and lovely with broad winding paths and expansive vistas overlooking the Hungarian countryside. Once we reach the bottom of the mountain, we sit together in an open-air chapel with a dirt floor and split a candy bar. Plastic sleeves stapled to the trees encase photographs of those who saw visions here. Condensation collects inside the plastic, smearing the pictures into abstraction. A couple hiking with two Doberman Pinschers walk past, the dogs slobbering and breathing heavily, straining against the loops of their collars. As they walk away, their labored inhales and exhales resonate down the hill behind us and I wonder what those celestial visions must've looked like. Did the people pictured in the photos know that their vision was a message from beyond? Did they question their visions? I watch another couple meander through the chapel and take picture after picture, snapping images of a place famed for invisible revelations.

It is evening by the time we arrive at the Széchenyi baths, kept at 165 degrees Fahrenheit. The bathhouse is a Neo-baroque brilliant yellow with ornate flourishes of gold and white. The multiple outdoor pools glow aquamarine in the darkness. As Tiffany and I sit in the pool and watch the steam roll off the waters and disappear into the night, we discuss how *good* we will feel the next day after our day of cleansing, what *wonderful* things we are doing for ourselves, how this day has been perfect. Hairy, barrel-chested men lounge around the pool's perimeter, arms perched on the tiled edge. Rambunctious conversations in Hungarian reverberate around us. With the language's long vowels and melodic sentences even an argument sounds romantic to my unknowing ears. Steam fumes off visitors exiting the pool as they skitter toward the bathhouse, feet thwacking against the cold concrete. Meanwhile, Tiffany and I chatter about how this moment of watching water evaporate into air is mystical and magical and evidence of the universe's cosmic order, how watching steam disappear into the stars is like a metaphor for *life* and *death* and the possibility of *reincarnation*. We tell one another that this *whole day* is evidence of the universe's love and when we wake tomorrow, we will feel that unconditional love as our souls have been cleansed by the earth's own hands. *We will be magic!*

We stay until closing, until our fingers and toes have pruned beyond recognition, until we are dizzy and pink, until our eyes turn bloodshot from the steam, until we drift to the Metro station and take our respective trams home.

I awake the next morning with what feels like the most supreme hangover, a total sapping of my will to roll over in bed or get up to urinate or think in complete sentences. The twin mattresses provided by the school are more like siblings to your average box spring than anything close to a legitimate mattress. While I had never been entirely comfortable on my bed, despite having three of them and doing some extensive research to convince myself that sleeping on hard surfaces is beneficial for my skeletal alignment, this morning I feel as though I have melted and hardened in the night and awoke unable to move.

After planning for twenty minutes how to reach my phone, I half-slither off my bed with my torso on the floor and pick up the phone to call Tiffany to see if she feels freeze-dried. While inching off the bed, I theorize: *Was I drugged? Am I having an allergic reaction to something? The mineral water? The . . . crackers we ate? How could I feel this horrible from a hike and a glorified swimming pool?*

Flashback to high school home economics. When cooking chicken there is a hierarchy wherein some methods are preferable to others. Baking and broiling preserve the chicken's moisture and preserve any flavoring choices. Sautéing is an option for those of us skilled enough not to burn our chicken. Boiling is used only when no other method is available; it saps the meat of its moisture and results in a mound of stringy, tough, unappetizing flesh. I envision two pieces of raw meat spiraling in bubbling water on a stovetop. *There's Tiffany. And there's me.*

We've cooked ourselves. After calling to confirm this with her, I spend the rest of the day drinking tap water and crawling around my apartment.

The next day at school, my students ask what's wrong with me.

"You look very ill," says one freckled boy in the front row.

"Oh! I went to the baths over the weekend and I just stayed in a bit too long. I'm just a little dehydrated. I'm fine."

"How long did you stay in?" another student asks.

"Oh . . . I don't know. I guess, we were in there two-and-a-half, maybe three hours."

They gasp and in a spontaneous round robin-like chorus chirp back at me.

"Miz Kortinee! You stay in for twenty minutes only! Twenty minutes! Not hours! There is a sign! There is a sign that says it!"

I'd seen a sign, multiple signs around the pool, but Tiffany and I didn't pay any attention to them. We were watching steam roll into the stars. We were talking about life and love and cleansing our livers and the texture of our souls. *We were magic!*

I call my mother the next morning to tell her about the mountain and the baths. I relay to her what my students had said about the sign and about how long we'd stayed in the waters. I tell her that we'd "cooked ourselves like boiled chicken"—I assume she'll think this is funny.

Instead, she too gasps in response, says my full name, and exclaims, "You need to take care of yourself! If there's a sign there, *you need to read it.* And if it's in a different language, then you need to figure out what it says."

I hang the phone up.

I thought that's what I'd been doing this entire time.

Part Two

Retrograde Station

The celestial body hovers static, preparing to
backtrack; chaos, frustration, obstacle.

Holes

Your Reading For: December 14, 2012
Oh Aries! What delight! An opportunity for improving your domestic skills awaits! Detect our sarcasm? Look closer—there's nothing you can do. But trust there's nothing you could've done either.

My current mystery is the disintegration of my clothing. Over the past month, almost every piece of clothing I own has sprung a hole. I've researched European washing machines, looked up the properties of Hungarian laundry detergent, and asked the science teachers I work with if radioactivity can manifest itself in holes in fabric or if there is a species of insect or crustacean that is not only invisible and likes to eat clothing but is also fond of living in apartments with lead paint and four couches. Somehow these holes breathe the funk of something awful in my midst. Fantasies about vacant graves underneath my apartment, rabid moths chewing at the insulation, and impending massive molar cavities obsess me.

I decide to solicit help.

I call Donny.

He picks up.

"Hello?"

"Donny. It's your sister. What does the word 'hole' mean to you?"

"... Hole?"

"Hole."

"It's a band. A terrible band."

"Well, sure. But, think, like, holes in your socks or black holes in the sky—"

"Assholes! What about 'assholes'? That's what I think of."

I call friends who suggest that I stop shopping at thrift stores and check my closet for moths. My father tells me it's probably my washer.

I call my mother, the woman who might actually ponder the metaphorical, cosmic meaning of my disintegrating wardrobe.

I dial and listen to the phone trill until the answering machine picks up.

Record your message after the beep.

I leave a message, "It's urgent, Mom! Messages are afloat! HOLES. Holes everywhere! We need to discuss this—call me back!"

No reply.

Two weeks pass, and I *record my message after the beep* × fourteen. There is no response × fourteen.

I start a list of theories: *They've abandoned all technology. They've taken a spontaneous vacation. They think this is funny. Unbeknownst to me, I've done something awful and they're shunning me . . .*

I call again. The fifteenth call and it's—

Record your message after the beep.

On day sixteen, I call Bruce's office and *record my message after the beep.*

On day seventeen, I call again and before I can *record my message after the be—*

She answers.

I perch in the armchair, my heart pounding, giddy to hear her voice, and ask how she is.

". . . Me?"

"Yes . . . of course. How are you? I've been calling."

She tells me she's just about to go to a doctor's appointment and giggles hysterically.

The line goes silent.

"Mom?"

I wait, listening to the connection crackle.

She tells me about visions—strange visions, the beautiful images she sees each morning while she lies in bed and looks out the window. She tells me a story about the dragonflies that follow her around and the pets that we've never kept. *Buster the dog,*

Alexander the lizard, Kissie the kitten. She met—no, yes, *yes.* She *met* a seizure and she went to see the gynecologist . . . no. No, not that. She went to see an . . . *oncologist* and he had bad news for her.

"What's the news?" I ask, finding the hole in my shirt and tugging on it.

I listen to the static. I listen for her breath.

"What's the news?" I ask again, plunging my fingers into the hole and ripping until I fit my whole hand inside.

My mother tells me that she is terminally ill. She has six months, or less, to live.

I ask her if she's lying to me.

And she says, no . . .

No, she's not.

This is it. She's, you know, *dying* . . .

I am seized.

I keep ripping and ripping, listening to the fabric shred, asking questions that she doesn't answer, until all that's left is dial tone and the memory of that psychic at the bar, that afternoon I had forgotten about without hesitation, an afternoon I had held up as mystical mockery.

I take off my shirt, rip along the seams, up to the armpits, along the sleeves, around the collar, and toss it on the floor.

Numbness settles over me.

I stand up and pace around the room.

Rabid moths? Cavities? Shopping at garage sales?

None of that.

I charge back to the chair with the intention of calling Tif— *Tiffany is a motherless daughter. A motherless daughter who befriended me* . . . Is this a coincidence? Or a moment of cosmic matchmaking? *Cosmic matchmaking.*

My numbness evaporates and I am all rage. What does this mean? Why did the one forecast I tossed off actually manifest itself? Why was my mother talking about her ashes being thrown into the lake just a year ago? Why would she even say that? Why did my *father* talk about my mother dying just a few months ago? Do the holes have anything to do with this? And if they did, how was that supposed to help anything? What is the point of any of this? I turn to the wall and press my back against it. Sliding to the floor, I close my eyes, and wait for my next daily reading.

Viszontlátásra!

Your Reading For: December 29, 2012
     Well, little Ram, take a good look at that suit-
case of yours. What can fit? Not much. But there's
no need to worry. Focusing on the material will
only give you more to carry.

Goodbye Budapest. Goodbye beached whale. Goodbye slab bed. *Szia* goulash. *Viszlát* handfuls of Túró Rudi candy. Goodbye metro trips. Goodbye hours roaming along pastel fences. Goodbye traipsing through art nouveau architecture. *Viszontlátásra* students—so sorry, I have to leave. Goodbye job— I'm quitting. Goodbye Tiffany—I'll see you back home. Goodbye Hungary; I have to go. Goodbye European adventure; I've booked my flight: Budapest to Barcelona to New York to Minneapolis and back to This Place.

But first, I have thirty-six hours in Barcelona and I take it. I take the bus downtown. I take a locker to shove my luggage in. Take a photo of my aura and I'm a woman in an electric fog— frenzied, trembling, feeling as though tectonic plates shift and collide within me. I take a map and feel those plates crash, my chest tight. I take another map. I take the Gran Via de les Corts Catalanes. I take the Plaça de la Universitat. I take the Ronda de Sant Antoni. I take the Carrer de Viladomat. I take the possibility that the store I pass by advertising *tienda esotérica y tarot* is what I think it means. I dart toward the entrance and upon first sniff of frankincense and sage, I know what this place is and feel a small trickle of levity edge through those plates. There are silk scarves hung from the ceiling and foot-long crystal points behind the counter and a poster showing an auric body and I take a basket as those plates back slide again, levity destroyed, my hands tight in fists around the handles. I take my panic and pacify myself with the possibility that these chakra-themed candles will soothe me and put them in the basket. I take my throat, so tight it might snap, and think that this handful of rocks will, of course, be useful. I take and take hoping that these items will act as caulk and flatten the crevices where I am ripping. I take some essential oils and a big salt rock and ask the clerk where the books are.

"Miss, they—are—um, all in Spanish."

"That's okay. I'd just like to see them. Please. *Gracias.*"

She shows me. And, yes, they are all in Spanish but I see titles with *astrología* and *espiritualidad* and toss a few in my basket. I can't read them, but they've been sitting in this esoteric shop long enough that their very pages might be infused with the sort of soul-lifting energies I need. Into my basket they go and back around the store I whirl.

Finding my way back toward the cashier, I stop and rummage through the accumulated items. Tarot cards of all varieties, rocks upon rocks, incense to last me the rest of this decade, books about— what am I doing? I don't need this stuff, I don't need any of it. I have no room in my luggage. I have no way to lug this back home. But I feel those plates grind. My lungs pinch. I tremble. I am scared. My guide is gone—dying. She has terminal brain cancer, an abnormal mass the size of a peach pit nestled in her skull. That supposedly psychic man at the bar five years ago was right—but what was the point of his prediction? It came true. But now what? Had my mother taken his prediction seriously could she have prevented this? Or is this part of her path, our path? What's the point of divination if the future still occurs no matter how horrible or fabulous the prediction? Have I invested my beliefs and time into ideas that are ultimately fruitless?

I look down at the items in my basket.

I am a buffoon.

I am an idiot.

I am totally lost.

I start hurriedly shoving everything back on the shelves, grabbing items by the fistful and cramming them onto display cabinets.

The clerk stops me.

"Uh, miss—do you need any help?"

Yes! Of course I do—just look at me! I'm quaking! Crumbling! Weeping! How do I stop these plates shifting? What can I trust? What am I supposed to *do* now that my—

"No. No. I'm fine. Thank you—*Gracias* . . ."

I look into the basket. "Oh, actually . . ."

I take three rocks from the basket: a pink quartz, an amethyst, and a green aventurine.

"I'd like to purchase these. For my mother. Please."

The clerk takes them behind the counter. I stand and wait, my basket empty, doubt bubbling in, foaming at my fissures, pushing from every angle of my being.

I take my mother's stones, put them in my pocket, and walk out of the shop. I shuffle toward the smell of fish and salt and take the Moll de les Drassanes. I take the Rambla de Mar and walk onto the boardwalk and listen to the sound of my boots scuffing the wooden planks.

I take a seat and look out onto the undulating Balearic Sea.

Pigeons strut and fight over pizza crusts and abandoned pretzels, feathers shimmering green and purple in the sunlight. Chest heaving and tender, I turn to watch the water and wonder if I can continue to soothe myself in the murky, mystical waters of the Deep End. I wonder if it is time to retreat to shore.

I take the rocks out of my pocket and squeeze them.

I turn my gaze to the horizon and for the first time since I shoved those tarot cards in my mother's purse as a girl, I see the Deep End sprawling before me as simultaneously alluring and eerie.

WELCO

Your Reading For: January 3, 2013
  Now, now, baby Ram. Yes, it's a tragedy, right?
  Dry your tears and take your cue from the migrat-
  ing mergansers. Know that your stay is temporary.

My father and Donny pick me up at the Minneapolis
airport where I meet them in baggage claim carrying
a duty-free bag of chocolates: truffles stamped with Mozart's face,
tiny Kinder chocolate bars, Hungarian Sport chocolate that tastes
like licking an exposed brick wall, Swedish gummy candies, and
iron-infused Lithuanian Hematogenu candy bars rumored to have
calves' blood in them.

I've brought distractions.

As we cross the Minnesota-Wisconsin border, I sit in the backseat of my father's truck, open the chocolates, and hand different
pieces to my father and Donny in the front seats. The WISCONSIN
WELCOMES YOU sign blurs past us. The traffic noticeably slows as
the number of Minnesota plates around us dissolve into Wisconsin
plates chugging east.

My father's hyped up in showtime mode. It's nearly midnight
and he's awake! The radio is cranked! He has a captive audience!
He tells stories about eating desserts in Iceland where he hunted
puffins last year and composing a letter that was probably written
in ALL CAPS to a boat salesman he got in an argument with last
week. He laughs his booming laugh and looks at Donny and turns
back to look at me more than he looks at the road. He opens the
window and spits a masticated glob of a Sport bar out onto the
highway and tells it that it's a piece of shit as he closes the window.

And as the lights of rest stops and gas stations and bars dotted along the highway glide past and I listen to the two of them rant in the front seat, my mind turns images over and over again. I think of the last moment I hugged my mother in August before I left. I think of the holes in my socks, my sweaters. I think of my shirt lying in scraps on the floor. I think of that psychic from five years ago. That ring he made me—should we have listened? How could we have known? *Rewind, repeat.* My mother's hair in my face, the sun beating against us in the August heat. The shirt ripping. Those baby carrots I brought with me. But we *did* know. Could we have done something? *Rewind, repeat.* My mother's arms around my waist. We should've done something. Why didn't we? I shoul—

"Hey, Court!" Donny yelps from the front.

"What?"

"Hand me the rest of that hema-tengetous or whatever shit."

I hand him the Lithuanian candy bar and my father sings along to Foreigner on the radio, pounding the beat on the steering wheel with his hand, "Cold as ice! Bah bah duh dah! Ooo . . ."

We arrive at my mother's house.

Inside the living room, someone has taped a WELCOME HOME! sign to the far wall. The WELCO letters are still taped to the wall but the ME HOME! letters of the strand dangle by a piece of twisted tape straining to hold onto the plaster wall.

My father puts my luggage down and stalks off to the bathroom while Donny looks at the paper chain and mutters, "I never got a fucking banner."

The sound of my father peeing reverberates throughout the house.

Donny wheels around to roll his eyes at me.

"Shut the door!" Donny hisses in the bathroom's direction.

The stream cuts off. The door slams, suspended letters twirl.

I bound down the stairs to my bedroom, push open the door, and find the space as I left it in August. Bedspread cockeyed across the mattress, pillows flattened and wrinkled, the floor unswept, a spider web wafting against the ceiling. I drop my backpack near the door, crawl on top of the covers, and think of my mother sleeping on the floor above me, her little face nestled among pillows. I imagine running up the stairs to greet her the next morning. I imagine her walking to me, arms outstretched. I imagine the feeling of her embrace and the thought of it alone lulls me to sleep.

Star Shit

Your Reading For: January 4, 2013

You must remember: everyone is working with the amount of light they have. And some may occasionally need a flashlight.

The sign has fallen in the night. Snow glares through the lake-facing windows as the letters sit heaped and silhouetted against the stark landscape. Squinting, I creep up the stairs and read the pile—the M mashed into the CO, the W pinned underneath the ME, the EL sticking straight up. *MmmcoWuhMe.* I rub my eyes.

The coffeemaker murmurs. It's 8:07. Bruce is already out the door and gone, traversing the slick roads to work. Languid, I shuffle to the kitchen, mystified by the sheer volume of fruit baskets and crescent rolls and oily muffins that have never occupied these countertops before; pour a cup of coffee; and turn around to slouch against the countertop as a figure—a woman, face bloated and jaundiced, hair tangled, shoulders hunched; a woman dressed in faded pink thermal underwear and oversized wool socks—shuffles past, looks at me, considers my face for a moment, turns her back, and strolls into my mother's bedroom.

Who—? What? Wait—

That was my mother.

"Mom?" I ask to the empty kitchen.

"Mom?" I yell past the kitchen to the living room.

I set the coffee cup in the sink and bolt to her room.

I hold my hand up to knock and—

The rocks . . .

I run downstairs, find the rocks, go back to her door, and knock, "Mom? I'm home! I brought you something."

Blankets and sheets shuffle. The bed creaks.

I turn the handle, open the door, and scan the room. Sage-colored walls remain sparse. Dust collects on the windowsill looking out to the lake. My mother's slippers sit kicked into a corner. The bedspread drapes with a distinctive lump lying still beneath.

Hair sticks out from the covers in a cockatiel flourish.

"Mom?"

The lump is silent.

Does she recognize me?

"Mom? It's me. Courtney. Your daughter?"

The lump remains still.

Was she sleepwalking?

I go to the opposite side of the bed and crawl in. Finding her underneath the covers, I hug her. She's all strain and sweat, unyielding to touch.

"Mom? Can you hear me?"

Breaking from my embrace, she whips the covers off her.

"Yes—Courtney. I hear you."

I sit up, frantic and enthralled. She spoke. She can hear me. She recognizes me. I watch as she pulls herself up.

"You didn't have to come back."

". . . I wanted to be here with you."

My palms are swamps, the stones wet and slippery. I am all taught and tension; I can see myself nearly giving into the weight of this pressure and melting, a plastic figurine tossed into a bonfire and shriveling. I have never before longed so much for her approval, her embrace, her validation.

"I—I brought you a present. From Barcelona."

Trembling, I get out of bed, stumble to my mother's side, sit on my knees, and present the rocks to her in my outstretched hand.

She extends her limp left hand and I place the stones in it.

"These are for you."

She looks at them.

". . . You bought me rocks?"

"They're—*gemstones.* I bought them for you. They'll help you. They're—you know, for your heart and your—health."

She stares at them and I can't take the silence. I start to babble, "I got them just for you. I went to this special shop. You would've really liked it and I almost bought a bunch of other stuff and then I didn't and. So. You know. I thought you'd like them, because, you and I—"

She outstretches her hand in a fist.

She looks at me.

She shakes her fist, eyes fixed on mine.

I tentatively open my palm and she places the rocks back in my hand and I am plastic. I am shriveling. I am engulfed in flames.

She sinks back into the covers.

"You should've brought booze. That would've been more helpful."

I am gone.

I slink back downstairs, burst into Donny's room, flip the light on, and shake him awake. Donny's been home since December but it looks like he's been living in this room for months and has never emerged—it's an absolute mess: dirty sweatshirts and socks scattered, papers and schoolbooks hastily stacked in the corner, beer bottles collecting next to the bed. Donny, now twenty-one, is taking his university courses online this semester so he, too, can be home.

"Donny, wake up! Wake up, Donny!"

"Courtney, stop—stop it! What is wrong with you?"

He sits up in bed and rubs his eyes. I grab his stubbled chin and force him to look at me.

"What. Is. Wrong. With. Mom?"

He knocks my hand away, gawking at me.

"I mean—besides the *obvious*?"

"Donny! I just went up there—and—she—she didn't even seem to *recognize* me. She's—completely different, Donny! What is going on?"

"She's dying, Court." He rubs his eyes again.

"I *know* that, Donny!"

"I mean—Courtney. I don't know. She just got this really fuckin' awful news. How is she supposed to act?"

"I don't know, Donny! I just—I left in August and she was our mother. And I don't even know *who* that was!"

"Court . . . I don't know what to tell you. I've been here for the past month and this is how it's been. She doesn't say much. She doesn't do much, jus' sits in her room. This is just how it is."

"But—Donny. What—what . . ."

He looks at me, his face vacant.

"Donny, she's our *mother*. And she was my *guide* and *confidant*—I don't know what I'm supposed to do, how I'm supposed to be."

The heater kicks on and blows lukewarm through his bedroom. He's still staring at me, his eyes puffy and crusted.

"I feel . . . lost, Donny. I feel blindsided and sad and . . . *afraid*. I am afraid of the *future*, Donny. I'm afraid and I don't know what to do. And she's our *Mom*. And I've spent my whole life just running to her, running to her for help and guidance and now—"

"Go look at your star shit."

". . . My star *shit*?"

"Yeah, your star shit."

"Donny! I looked at my *star shit* and the star shit told me—us—that this was gonna happen and look what good that did us! I knew! I *knew* and it happened anyway!"

Donny crawls out of bed.

"Well, Court. None of that shit is her *job*. She already fuckin' raised you. If you can't figure out what the fuck to do, then I guess you're S.O.L."

He stalks out of the room.

Donny's feet plod across the kitchen floor above as panic expands inside me. *But the star shit is all I have . . .*

I spend the rest of the day cross-legged on the floor of my bedroom awash in dread-fueled divination as I ask question after question, inquiry after inquiry, scrutinize worry after worry. I lay tarot card after tarot card down. I concentrate on questions and watch a pendulum swing clockwise and counterclockwise and back-and-forth. I throw coins and ask questions from the I Ching, an ancient Chinese divination method. I look at planetary transits and Moon cycles and Pluto's path. And the message that reflects back illustrates what is already apparent: *This is a time of relationships ending, a death is possible, this is the end of a cycle, this is a time of separation and pain, this is your task—let go from that which you have clung to . . .*

But the dread continues to steep and I continue to ask more questions—the same questions I asked before phrased in different ways, hoping to get a different response, hoping I was asking incorrectly or I wasn't specific enough the first time.

In response, the tarot shows me the Devil card with a man and a woman chained at his hairy feet again and again. *You are engaging in negative thinking. Obsessions prevail! Are you indulging in alcohol, drugs, or pessimism?* The I Ching shows me Hexagram Four again and again. *Mountain over water: You do not get to know. You have asked too many questions. You cannot know right now.* The pendulum hangs still, ignoring my pleas.

I wrap a rubber band around the tarot cards and lob them into the corner.

Yes, Devil card, I am engaging in obsessions and pessimistic thinking. Yes, I Ching, I have asked too many questions. And yes, pendulum, I understand why you hang still—there is nothing left to say. But, you—tarot cards, I Ching coins, pendulum, astrology charts, my *star shit*—you are the only ballast I have to cling to.

And I am clinging with everything I have.

As I crawl into bed that night, the rocks meant for my mother clasped to my chest, the moonlight reflects off the snow and through my bedroom window the land glows. I lie awake until two, staring at the luminous snow and onward into the expansive sky, and think about those planetary bodies whose messages urge me to surrender. I lie awake and think about the repeated readings offering no future outcomes but only present clarifications, urging me to examine what *is* rather than what will be. I lie awake and wonder if I can abandon my need to know, my need to have a guarantee, if I can trust in the Deep End's enigmatic path. I lie awake and wonder who I will be without my mother and who I would be if I were to leave the Deep End behind. Would I be anyone at all?

I lie awake and wonder why we have so many fruit baskets.

Moses

Your Reading For: January 7, 2013

Ah, yes! Should've checked twice before you left Budapest, right? But how could you have known that you left your phrasebook underneath the third bed? So much furniture in that little space! No worries, impetuous one, trust that you already know how to translate.

It's midnight. Donny is supposed to be studying for a marketing test. Donny is supposed to be writing a paper about fruit fly reproduction. Donny is supposed to be reading about contemporary trends in public relations. But Donny shoved his books underneath the kitchen table days ago and has been slaying electronic extraterrestrials. He's been driving a remote control monster truck around the driveway and crashing it into snow banks. He's been wearing his hockey padding around the house and throwing tennis balls against the garage wall. And now, as I sit at the kitchen table reading about the transits of Pluto—planet of death, hospitals, and transformative destruction—Donny is hungry.

He disappears behind the refrigerator door and emerges with a plastic bag. He pulls it open, looks inside, and pokes his head up in horror.

"Who the fuck gave us seven pounds of cheese curds?" he asks.

"Jerry."

Jerry, Bruce's friend from Reno, bequeathed us yesterday seven pounds of curds: two white, two yellow, three jalapeño.

"Why the fuck did he give us seven pounds of cheese curds?"
Because, Donny, this is the language we must speak.

We speak the language of cheese curds. We speak the tongue of rhubarb pie and red velvet cake and blueberry cobbler. We understand the inner world of wild rice soup and gumbo. We have long chats with inspirational posters and stuffed animals holding hearts and a twenty-seven-pound Bible. We greet obscene amounts of chocolate on a daily basis. We understand the words spoken by waterproof mascara and those tiny packages of tissues.

We even understand the dialogue between the cheese cultures, the salt, the *whey*, and the *way* the seven pounds of cheese curds sit in the fridge, so innocent and humble and plastic-clad, between the pie, the tater-tot casserole, and the salmon dip. They all speak a language translatable by no one—not even the cheese curds themselves. It's the language of not knowing what to say, not knowing what to do, but watching a car crash and throwing a copy of *The Greatest Hits of Donny Osmond* toward the scene believing it will help.

Donny pops the cheese into his mouth curd-by-curd, gawks at me, and waits for an answer.

"I dunno know, Donny. It must've seemed like it would be . . . comforting."

I turn back to my book and Donny turns back to the fridge. A pile of newspaper horoscope clippings sits next to me, chronicling the last month up to today. I decided to start keeping evidence, credible or otherwise, of what's happening astrologically. I spent most of the afternoon digging through our recycling and clipping out the readings. I theorized that if I read them like a novel, one after another, there might be a message revealed only to those who try this method, if I prove that I will try even the most desperate measures, the universe will take pity on me and tell—

"What the hell are those?" Donny asks, pointing to my horoscope stack.

"My *star* shit, Donny," I reply.

He rolls his eyes, mouth open and chewing.

Despite your average citizen giving the pink slip to anything having to do with interpretations, signs, or symbolic messages, we're all mystics when we mourn in the Midwest. We interpret the fruit baskets and the daises and take them as a symbol. We won't say a word about the dying woman, but here's a linen-scented candle. We won't talk about death, but here's a box of Florida oranges. We won't weep before you, but here's a Bundt cake.

As Donny heats up a bowl of meatballs, I stare at the kitchen countertop lined with the well-meaning gifts of sympathy and condolences and wonder if this is where the woo-woo wisdom of the Midwest resides, our silences and emotional mysteries manifest in party trays and twelve-packs.

An hour later, after meatballs and the chapter on Pluto, after three beers and the chapter on Neptune, after more speculation as to *why* seven pounds of cheese curds—*What would anybody do with that many cheese curds?*—it's my turn at the fridge. I open the freezer and find four plastic wrapped slabs.

What?

I examine the slabs. They're all labeled. They're all—

"Banana Bread? We have four loaves of banana bread?" I ask.

My mother would never eat banana bread. She was not a banana bread woman. She was not an inspirational poster woman or a let's sit down and snuggle with a stuffed animal woman. She was also not a *pie* person. Pie was something that never happened. She was that let's get drunk and flash our relatives kind of woman. She was a saltines and Cheez-Whiz for dinner kind of girl. She mocked sentiment and shushed tears; her emotional world was an enigmatic Bermuda triangle.

"Yep—a bunch of it. All came from different folks. Bruce just stuck 'em all in there," Donny replies.

I shut the freezer door.

Yet if there was ever a time for our mother to be sentimental, to indulge in the cream puffs she denied herself for the sake of that paisley bikini, to slice up banana bread and bask in the glory of being alive, this was it. But the only message reverberating from her is: *none of this is touching me*—not the cards, not the letters, not the bears holding hearts, or the misty relatives ringing the doorbell.

As Donny fills the sink with hot water and soap and starts to toss dirty forks into the growing foam, I think about how I feel like apologizing to every person who has reached out to our mother only to receive a blank stare or the sound of her bedroom door closing at their arrival. When another pie, casserole, or loaf shows up with a visitor's weary smile, I internally rehearse a never-spoken spiel. *She really appreciates your thoughtfulness and the Bundt cake you brought. We all do. It's very kind of you. You have to understand her reticence—she's just processing. It's tough news. We have to give her grace. She's just not as emotive as she used to be right now.*

I turn away, shuffle to the sofa, flop belly-down, and breathe in the dusty upholstery.

Behind me, Donny scrubs the plates. They clink and tinkle against one another underneath the suds. The Sylvers' "Boogie Fever" plays on the radio and Donny dances along. His stockinged feet patter against the wooden floor. He dances back and forth, crooning and scatting. The dishes clink and clank. His feet hop and tap—and then Donny screams. Donny's screaming and I'm up and I'm looking around the kitchen. And I'm up and I'm looking and there's nothing there. It's just Donny cowering behind the sink looking out the window. And now I'm looking out the window and it's a face outside the window. A little ghostly face outside the window jiggling the sliding porch door. A little ghostly face attached to a little ghostly body trying to shove the door open. A little ghostly body and Donny is screaming and—

"Donny—it's *Moses*," I hiss.

Donny straightens up.

"What?" he asks.

"*Moses*—the next-door neighbor."

"Fucking *Moses*? Fucking *Moses* is on the porch at 1 a.m.?!"

Moses Sperling is our ninety-year-old neighbor with severe Alzheimer's who often tromps over here in the evening confused about where he is, where his parents are, and when he's supposed to go to school. He's never tried to break in before, though.

Moses starts to press his body against the door, as though it would open from pressure alone, and I run over to let him in. I unlock the door and slide it open, the cold air hitting me like a slap.

"Hi! Hi, Moses—what's going on?"

He stomps into the house disheveled in long underwear and green rain boots, a Navy anchor tattoo shriveled on his right forearm. Moses looks at me and ignores my question, snowflakes caught in his eyebrows. I can nearly feel Donny glaring at me, willing me to shut him back out.

Moses' teeth start to chatter.

"Jus' stay here for a second, Moses," I say to him.

I grab a blanket and wrap it around him while Moses chatters in full autobiography stream. He's not sure how he got here, but, you know, he goes to Holy Ghost Elementary School up on the hill and he was in the Navy. Then, you know, he worked at Uniroyal Tire Company for, oh, about thirty-five years.

"Do you know where my parents are? They're supposed to pick me up," he tells me.

"Well, I don't know where they are, Moses. But let's just go home. It's late."

Meanwhile, Donny has hoisted himself up on the countertop to fume.

"We should call the *cops*," he hisses to me.

I shrug, grab a flashlight, and lead Moses to the front door. As I turn around to shut the door behind me, I see her—my mother illuminated by a reading light, sitting in the spare room next to the front door. Snuggled underneath a red flannel blanket, she reads a thick paperback novel with the Eiffel Tower on the cover.

I look again.

When did she slip in? Has she been here this whole time? Did she hear us? Is this a mirage? A grief-induced delusion, a figment of a neurotic mi—

"Mom?"

She looks up, pink and flushed.

"Hi, Court," she whispers.

The front door still swung open by my hand, winter air streams through the door so cold it feels wet. I feel it on my face, my ears. My nose starts to run.

"What—what are you doing?"

"Reading." She looks at the cover, "About a woman in Paris."

"Oh, okay."

I stare, luxuriating in her presence. She turns the page and continues reading.

I smear my nose against my sweatshirt, whisper goodbye, link my arm with Moses', and walk out the front door. We trudge across the snow to his stoop.

The front door hangs open and I hustle Moses inside. Moses' house is laid out like an emporium of US Navy memorabilia and Victorian dolls—all of which haven't been touched since his wife's death in 1992. Orange shag carpeting sprawls through the house. The dolls stare indifferently as I lead Moses to his bedroom. I flip the lights on all the way, down the foyer, through the living room, up the stairs, down the hallway, and to his bedroom as Moses argues with me, "We don't need these lights on. Gotta keep 'em off. Mom and Dad are gonna know I'm late."

I lie. I keep flipping the lights on and I tell him I'll talk to his parents for him; I'll let them know what happened and that we had to turn the lights on and why we had to come home so late.

His arguments evaporate when I flip the lights to his room and exhaustion or mere habit leads him wordlessly back to bed.

I stand in the doorway and flip the lights off.

As I tiptoe back through the house, flipping the light switches off, the Victorian dolls' stoic faces glow in the darkness, fleeting orbs disappearing behind me.

I shut the front door tight and wait on Moses' stoop to make sure he doesn't escape to traipse along the lake bank or back over to our front door. I shuffle to stay warm and swear that it must have been a minor miracle that Donny and I happened to be up when Moses decided to break in through the backdoor. If we hadn't been there, would he have waited? Would we have found an icicle-crusted Moses in the morning? Or would he have gone home? A plane blinks above me, heading to Minneapolis or Fargo. After fifteen minutes, I trudge back across the property line and home.

The front door creaks open. My mother has gone to bed, her body's imprint vivid in the blanket, her book overturned. I walk toward the love seat where she read and feel the questions I have carried stir within me. I think of their numbers, their urgency, the seeming impossibility of their being answered. As I fold her blanket, I imagine myself suspended, lulled in the present, unable to find resolve; all of us waiting pendulums.

Don't—Tell—Dad

Your Reading For: January 17, 2013
Oh, little Ram, get over it! Yes, it's mortifying to bawl everywhere as though you're really an oyster, sloshing around in your own sauce all the time. But do not be so self-obsessed as to think that you are the axis point of anyone's universe but your own.

Donny has run into my room and collapsed face-down on my comforter.

"I don't—understand. I—don't. *Why*—why?" he says into the bed.

My brother is a bulimic crier. He'll stew for hours listening to Simon and Garfunkel and watch *Titanic* twice and pound seven shots before purging the entirety of his sadness at the foot of my bed. Holding him, a mere speck in my hands, I whisper, "You don't have to do this. You can just be sad and *not* watch *Titanic*. You're enabling yourself. You're digging yourself into The Pit when you don't—"

"I don't—care. I wanna be—in—The Pit. I wannit."

It was our new code: The Pit.

A few evenings earlier, while Donny shaved his head in our bathroom, I told him about the theater games I played as a teenager. We would sit in a circle, pass around a gutted chili pepper, and dab the innards under our eyes to try to make ourselves cry; a bag of onions sitting in the corner on stand-by. We'd smear menthol on each other's faces and stage complex sleights of hand with eye-drop bottles hidden in jean pockets. While waiting for class to start, we'd yawn and yawn, trying to eke out a leak. We spent hours in front of the mirror honing tortured Halloween mask faces, a muscle-memory technique intended to evoke previous tears cried for skinning your knee or seeing the neighbors' dog bloody and broken in the street or hearing the gunshot that killed Bambi's mother. A mascara smear on your cheek was a prize. That moist wad of Kleenex, a trophy. Crying was an art, a thing to be applauded. We'd whisper to each other, "Did you see Becky in that scene? *She cried.* Real tears. They were *real.*"

For us, crying was the hard part.

And dying was the fun part.

In one game we played, there were two roles—the one who kills and the one who dies. The weapon was chosen: laced vodka gimlet, meat cleaver, tank of piranhas, pistol, flesh-eating arctic animal. The one who was about to die would wait, lusting to be thrust into that tank of piranhas. Because this was the big show. This was *the* performance. And those in the audience—us— would be watching—envious, itching, wishing that we were the one about to be mauled by a leopard seal.

The stabbing, the lacing, whatever the pantomimed crime—it was a perfunctory thing, the safety demonstration before the flight takes off. The actual slaying was something you had to endure in order to be entertained. *Release the leopard seal, grab the meat cleaver—let's get to it.*

Dying always seemed to take a long time. Lots of heavy breathing and choking and flopping around and curses screamed at ex-roommates and "I love you and I never told you" and false-endings and hands reaching up toward the ceiling and digging yourself into the floor before becoming stiff and quiet.

And none of us would move.

Then we would clap. A standing ovation. Someone would whisper, "I hope *I* get to die next!"

The last game I told Donny about was played in a room with four corners. One corner was sadness, one corner was happiness, the third was boredom, and the fourth corner was anger. The middle was lust. The players were free to gravitate between the spots and "feel" the assigned emotion at their own pace. When I watched this game, what happened in the corners was predictable. The angry people kicked the wall and the bored people counted the stucco pimples on the ceiling and the happy people whistled. The middle had lots of lateral pole-dancing and moaning. But the sadness corner was what I remembered the most. Those who went there stayed there. Shoulders collapsed and heads drooped. Tears would drip. The students would cry and cry. It was like a pit they fell into. It seemed like they couldn't leave once—

Donny put the electric razor down, "Holy shit, Court. You're right—sadness is a fucking *pit*. You just fall in and you can't get out!"

We adopted The Pit as our mutual space, the place you go when grief wraps her arms around you and refuses to let go. Donny and I went in together to make sure that we both came out, like leashes parents put on their children at Disney World. There were rules in The Pit. We couldn't both be falling apart. One had to play therapist, to be calm, to hand tissues to the other.

Bruce was a diet crier. *Tears deLite!*© *Super Slim Sobs!*© He'd smoke cigarettes instead of crying, his tears adequately soaked up by a Q-tip. He was dainty in his grief. Wailing on the kitchen floor? Breakdowns inside restaurant bathroom stalls? Blotchy and quivering at 11 a.m.? *No, no. That's too much. It's not on my plan.* In the basement, we'd hear Bruce in the kitchen during the early morning hours, shuffling around and unpacking everything from his lunchbox that he'd refused to eat at noon. We would awake the next morning to see his carnage of ice cream containers, Hostess wrappers, and a single, empty scotch bottle left like a leper on the kitchen countertop and shamed by the daylight, Bruce's grief a secret.

Mine was not. I was the traveling "Girl Who Couldn't Stop Crying!" sideshow, an accidental exhibitionist. Donny could stuff it down, Bruce could tally it up to indulge in later, but I couldn't *not* cry. Sobbing in public became as banal as a sneeze. I cried everywhere I went—birthday parties, the gynecologist's office, between library stacks.

In spite of tears, "Carrying on" was my war cry, the thing to convince me that life hadn't completely bottomed out from underneath us, my message: "EVERYTHING IS TOTALLY FINE. I mean, LOOK AT ME. I weigh oranges at the supermarket! I buy commemorative stamps! I complain about potholes in the street! OBVIOUSLY, I'M FINE." I was horrified by the monstrosity of wailing, my continual stream of snot, my abs sore from lamenting and sighing, my ever-present puffy face. I sometimes thought of myself as a public service announcement for people thinking about snorting vast amounts of cocaine, sky-diving with a shoddy outfitter, or eating superglue. *See this woman? See this hysterically crying woman? Don't turn the special people in your life into this woman.*

Our father was an in-denial crier, Mr. Macho Man. Me? *Cry?* Phfft. *Men don't cry.* He once tried to argue with me that men don't have "real" tear ducts past the age of twelve. He was not a wallower, not a "let's sit in The Pit together and I'll hand you Kleenex" confidant. If he could manufacture his own tissue brand, they'd be made of Brillo pads. You want pain? Here's pain— smear one'a these against your face.

Donny would often look up to me from the bottom of The Pit, choking and miserable and whisper, "Don't—tell—Dad."

Elvis

Your Reading For: January 29, 2013
Pretend you are a kite, young Aries. If you could see this situation from above, it would be clear. A mother wants her child to live their life—not watch hers disappear.

When you're dying and you know it, you actually do clap your hands. You and your immediate and not-so-immediate family and friends follow the instructions of some unproven but socially codified notion of what people are supposed to look like when the end is looming. The subtext of your daily existence reads as follows, *You need to make memories, dammit!* So you force yourself into the stuff of Chamber of Commerce brochures and after-school specials where everybody plays cards, talks about the 10:30 service over donut holes, and goes to seasonal theatrical productions. All the while, you smile like you're running for Senate, drink your decaf, and pretend that this is your everyday life. *We do this all the time! We love winter craft festivals! Are you kidding? We always go to the middle school choir concert!*

When all anyone really wants to do is disappear into their room, have a drink, smoke cigarette after cigarette, and/or kneel to sob into their knees. My mother's friends and coworkers loan us board games and DVDs. Friends suggest that my mother and I bake cookies together. We should knit. Play Scrabble. Make a scrapbook! *You can make some lasting memories! You'll remember the time you knit baby blankets with her when she's gone—it's important to do these things now.*

In the spirit of *making memories, dammit!* my mother's friend gave us tickets to see an Elvis impersonator at a nearby dinner theater with attached restaurant and motel.

The only way to get my mother to go to the craft fair or the luncheon with her sisters or the Elvis impersonator show is to make a mockery of the affair. I coax my mother into going to the Sunday matinee by smearing on burgundy lipstick and wearing fake fur the evening before and asking her if she'll be my date. The next day, I parade around in heels, false eyelashes, and a mink scarf while she brushes her teeth. I threaten to wear all of it *and* I tell her that I'm going to order champagne at the theater and take photos of the parking lot.

She says she'll go.

Once at the theater, we take our place in the back row of tables and I look out across the crowd of bused-in retirees from Sheboygan who've driven four hours to see their long-lost idol. My mother and I are the young buoys in a sea of gray-haired women, all of them scarved, perfumed, and bedazzled with cubic zirconia on their ears and fingers. Obvious skill and time had been put into their combed and sprayed helmet cuts and shiny press-on nails. Most are double fisting Bloody Marys and mimosas. Some have scarves specifically for the purpose of throwing or waving. All sit giddy, blushing, fluttering with anticipation as though we've really come to a hummingbird farm.

My mother elbows me in the back. I turn around to see her leaning against the wall, still wearing her winter coat, holding a cup of chamomile tea from the bar. Her hands tremble as she lifts the cup to her lips. Between her shaking and drinking tea and being at a kitschy dinner theater, the moment stings. I've never seen her so fragile, so ill, so distant. I've never seen her *drink tea* before.

She grimaces at the taste, sets the cup down, and mouths my name, *Courtney.*

I mouth back, *What?*

She stares at me. Her message: *What the hell are we doing here?*

I shrug. *Who knows!*

Though we both know— *We're making memories!*

The lights start to dim and Elvis jiggles onstage, Jail-House-Rock-ified. The audience shrieks. Women clap and dance in their seats. The theater is tiny, housing no more than sixty people. Elvis steps down from the wooden stage and the audience stretches their hands out to touch the King. The theater transforms into a coral reef, sea anemone tentacles extended and waiting for the impersonator to come past their row. I watch, torn between the possibility and impossibility of this situation—that someone you idolized and loved will return. That a singular body could be replicated. That a voice from the past could echo. That you could connect with what has been lost. The women shake their scarves and hoot as Elvis moves to the back of the audience. I breathe in—the air is hot and dry. I straighten my back against the wooden chair.

We're on the very end of the row. Elvis comes up to me first. He looks so young up-close, maybe thirty-five or six. His eyeliner already smeared, his stage make-up caked on his stubbled cheeks, he reaches his hand out toward me. I reach mine out to grace his calloused fingertips. He blows a kiss to my mother and meanders down the row reaching his hand to other audience members as my mother snorts and muffles a screech.

I turn around.

With one hand to her mouth, a laugh escapes, and then she can't hold back. She's shaking, her shoulders heaving; she's shrieking. I don't know if she's laughing at Elvis or at the screaming retirees or at this whole situation—being at an Elvis impersonator show while she's bald and pallid and dying—but whatever it is, she thinks it's hilarious. Meanwhile, Elvis has finished visiting our row and is back onstage. I turn around to watch him gyrate his hips back and forth. The lights figure-eight around and around. Elvis puts his thumbs inside his waistband. He shuffles, thrusts, and grins at the audience. Women are now throwing their cloth napkins from the brunch service onstage. I breathe out, angst pushing at me . . . *possibility* . . . *impossibility* . . . And I begin to make a list of my last resources for unlocking my mother's silence.

Pawn It

Your Reading For: February 2, 2013
Sometimes what is indecipherable isn't meant to be deciphered. If the path you traverse feels difficult, maybe it's time to turn around. Have you ever considered how difficult it would be for your mother to tell you anything about her death or the future? Picture yourself in her place and then you'll know the challenge she faces. You'll understand her silence.

The next day, I call my father to let him know I'm showing up at his house with a fruit basket. When I pull into the driveway of his split-level brick house, I see him through the window, sitting in his recliner wearing his "woodland" camouflage ghillie suit. He wears it for turkey hunting but the ensemble would also be an appropriate choice if you wanted to be a compost pile for Halloween. He waves. When I told him about my mother's diagnosis, he brought over a twelve-pack of Coors, three bottles of wine—two reds, one white—a box of Kleenex, and asked what he could do to help. I told him it would help me very much if he wore his ghillie suit in public one time, just for me. He asked me if wearing it around his yard would count.

I said yes.

I wave back, an avalanche of anticipation and anxiety mounting inside me. My father has known her for over thirty years. My father was married to her. Maybe he has insights and perspective on the situation. My father could help. My father can tell me what I need to know.

He moves from the chair to meet me outside.

In that ghillie suit, he looks like the sixty-year-old love child of John Denver and Chewbacca.

It's winter in Wisconsin and just above freezing which means it's warm. And when it's warm you loll around outside and watch your neighbors power-walking around the cul-de-sac, numb and giddy, in shorts. We sit in the driveway, open up the cellophane, and each take an orange. I watch my father peel the rind, dribble juice on his hands, and wipe the mess on his suit all the while I can hear the avalanche crack within me. It has begun. I'm gonna bawl. I'm gonna heave and weep my guts out right in my father's driveway. I'm gonna splay my sorrow out before my stony, wouldn't-shed-a-tear father. One of his black Labrador retrievers sits before us, her eyes eager for the orange.

"*Dad.*"

He looks up, and I know he knows we are on the verge of me howling into the sleeve of his ghillie suit in the driveway, surrounded by melting snowmen and cellophane, in front of all the neighbors who've crawled out for the sunshine.

He looks nervous. He's concentrating too hard on peeling that orange. His eyes dart, he and his daughter about to venture into the territory of all things *sentimental* and *vulnerable.*

I can't even speak. Tears begin their jaunt down my face, dribbling and dripping off my chin. My orange sits indifferently in my hands. He swallows, reaches inside the suit to hand me his handkerchief, and grabs my orange to peel it for me.

I press the handkerchief to my face and soak it in seconds. I shake not from the breeze but from the falling debris within me. I cannot breathe, not from the cold but from all that has crumbled and stirred in the fall. I feel alone and ashamed weeping in the presence of my father but I cannot make this avalanche stop and so I let myself crash.

"I talked to Donny—about this. But I think we feel—differently. But, I just wanna know—if you were dying—you would tell me things, right? I mean—there would be some final words or whatever—passed on?"

"Yeah. I mean, of course, I would do that."

"Then—why isn't Mom doing that? She's silent. She doesn't—say anything. She won't have a conversation."

He pauses and tosses the peel into the snow.

"I dunno." The dog grabs the peel. "I mean, you would think if you're dying you'd wanna give some last words to your kids, you know."

"Yes! Exactly! The stakes are—*high*. She doesn't even talk about—being sick. She says—nothing. *Nothing.* And I don't know what to do—without her. I feel desperate—to talk to her—while she's here."

The lab brings the peel back to him.

"I mean, Dad, do you think—she'll ever tell me—*anything?*"

"Maybe? Can she? Maybe she's too sick . . ."

"That's true . . ."

I start to shiver.

"But, do you think she'll tell me things in—you know—the afterlife? You know, beyond our world, she'll still—"

"Cork, you gotta let that shit *go*. You just have to live with things the way they are. You can't dream about these . . . you know, *imaginary* things."

The avalanche settles and crusts.

I feel weak.

He hands me my orange and sticks his legs out in front of him.

". . . But, what—what should I do, Dad? I need to talk to her."

"I dunno—she's your mother," he replies, popping an orange wedge into his mouth.

The neighbor lady jogs past us and waves.

My father waves.

I feel I might shatter if I move.

We finish our oranges in silence. I stand up and thank him for wearing the outfit and he stands up and thanks me for the fruit and hugs me lopsided, shoving my face in his armpit. Up close his swamp-creature-suit is fetid, like sticking your nose in between the cracks of a moist, abandoned barn. He asks me if wearing the ghillie suit made me feel better and I tell his armpit, yes, very much so, and he lets go. He disappears into the garage with the dog following behind. My teeth start to chatter. I walk back to my car, the words *imaginary things* plummeting through me.

I arrive home, lock myself behind my closet door, and crawl onto the floor.

I lie with my head on my forearms and gaze at the shelves along the wall, the wood floor cold. Esoteric books and adolescent treasures line the closet: glossy yearbooks, old diaries, letters from forgotten summer camp friends, and scratched CDs. I see the book about North Node and South Node astrology that my mother and I had read together when I was sixteen. I remember those words . . . *silence* . . . *doubt* . . .

I prop myself up and pick at a piece of dried orange rind on my thumbnail.

Silence . . .

What can I do if she simply refuses to speak to me? To anyone?

I look at the stack of yearbooks and diaries.

I could write her a letter.

I could write her a letter and tell her everything—my fears, my desires. I could get the words out and she could respond. Maybe writing would be easier for both of us.

I stand up, flip through an old spiral notebook, and find a blank page. I rip it out, lie belly down on the floor of my closet, and write the words that have stewed within me, but I can't get them down on paper.

I start a sentence and erase it.

I start a sentence and cross it out.

I poise the pencil and can't write.

I try to start again but the words read hollow. My desire for her to speak to me feels selfish. Why should I be demanding this of a dying woman? If she refuses to speak or respond, shouldn't that be the final word?

I rip out another page and write instead of my love, gratitude, and sorrow for her and invite her to write back.

I slip upstairs and leave the card next to her toothbrush so she'll see it the next day.

The following morning, I am surveying the bagel sampler Donny's friend gave us when my mother shuffles up behind me and touches my hand. "Thank you for the card, Courtney. That's very nice of you."

I inhale, tingling with anticipation of the letter she's going to pull from her robe or the kiss she'll smear on my cheek or the card she's going to hand me that's so sentimental it oozes at the creases.

She squeezes my hand.

"You can have all of my clothes."

She releases her grip and patters away, leaving me standing at the bagel sampler.

I exhale, my breath a whine.

As I watch her walk toward her bedroom, I am every song of unrequited love and it pounds through me like a subwoofer. And with each repeating chorus, I lose more hope of ever communing with her in earnest again.

Days later, while my mother sits at the kitchen counter reading the newspaper, I exercise my privilege as a daughter to borrow my mother's clothing. I am rooting through her wooden jewelry armoire when she walks up behind me and pats my back, her hand a feather.

I nearly jump.

"Mom?" I say, still facing the jewelry.

"Soon, Court, all of this will be yours. And then in twenty years, you can sell it or melt it down for cash."

"Mom!" I say, wheeling around. "I'm not gonna, you know, *melt* your stuff down or pawn it. I'll keep it and I'll wear it to—to remember you. I'll wear it to remember you."

She meets my eyes.

Hot-boxed in by her own demise, she knows the cards she holds, *step-by-step, this is how you will go.* Dumbfounded by the hand she's drawn, clutching to her fortune, her only certainty, she has let everything else go. The periwinkle robe that she's worn for weeks, swaddling her astonishing emaciation, is grimy with spilled coffee, urine, and melted chocolate. Losing scratch-offs sit crumpled in the pockets. This robe is her white flag. *Take me. I am weary.* Holding her gaze, I do not need a sign or message—I understand her mental chokehold, strangled by an unfathomable grip on a life still green.

A single tear forms in her eye and slides down her face.

We are silent.

"Mom. Why do all your friends think you like banana bread?"

Richard

Your Reading For: February 4, 2013
Young Ram! If you merely want to use the
Deep End as a tool for entertainment, just buy ro-
mance novels set by the sea. Otherwise, commit
and quit wavering. Riches come from immersion,
not oscillation.

Has the universe been listening to my pleas?
I've been cast in the local dinner theater's winter production performing at the same theater where we saw "Elvis." I get paid to pretend that I'm in love with my high school infatuation, Richard—which doesn't feel like pretending at all.

Richard is my brother's age and looks like John Lennon's lost son. He spends hours in his room writing tortured film scripts that never see the light of day. He listens to Polish electronica and only wears suits. He is beautiful and bizarre.

As a teenager, I would follow my mother around the house and gush over seeing Richard in the hallway or in his gym shorts during Phys. Ed. or at the—

"That boy is *weird*, Courtney. He's just *weird*."

"But he's an *Aquarius*, Mom. They're *all* weird."

Or Linda Goodman says, "To Aquarius, odd is normal. Normal is odd."

Richard was a model Aquarian.

My initial reading at age fourteen of his natal chart should've been taken as a warning that I could never seduce his Aquarian soul. But in typical Aries fashion, I took his coolness and disinterest as a sign that he was denying his true longings for me. I reasoned that if I was persistent, even if it took years, he would eventually be unable to resist my Aries prowess and we would bound off into a dreamy partnership as an astrologically sanctified union, yoked together by the planets.

When I saw the cast list, read the script, and realized we were playing a couple, I decided to re-examine our astrological compatibility. If we had been cast as a fictional couple did this mean that the universe was showing us we could be a *real* couple? But now, I had more than just Linda Goodman and clumsy chart readings. I could get into the innards of our relationship—I could really *know* by casting a synastry chart. A synastry chart shows the relationship between two natal charts; they are a helpful tool in determining compatibility of not only romantic relationships but any relationship.

Pulsing with the possibility of my long-lost adolescent heartthrob and me finally running into one another's arms, I cast the chart. But as I examined my chart with Richard, I saw this was not cosmic matchmaking. It was a cosmic backhand, a mystical reality check. Richard and me? We were never meant to be. There were too many squares involving Venus. There was too much friction, not enough attraction. Too much awkwardness, not enough ease. Most alarmingly, our chart had the sudden death marker of a relationship that is unrequited—our Moons, the sign of your emotional, inner world, didn't connect at all. The universe cast us as a fictional couple because all we would ever be was a fiction.

After consulting my books, I run to Donny's room, where he sits at the headboard of his bed staring at a marketing textbook's cover, and throw myself across his bed.

"I thought the universe was bringing us *together*!" I yowl, tossing a book about synastry charts at Donny. "Just *look* at it— it's bad! It's really bad! I marked all the spots."

Donny watches the book land with a dull thud next to him.

"Court, Richard is one of the strangest dudes I've ever met. You don't want *that*."

"Donny! You don't understand my lust! My DESIRE. My LONELINESS. I really do want him! It's been TEN YEARS. TEN YEARS of longing!"

I turn my face downward and breathe in something awful.

I sit up.

I'm sprawled on a mound of Donny's unwashed clothing that he heaved onto his bed after the garbage bag he'd thrown it in burst on his way to the laundry room.

"What *is* all of this?" I ask, looking straight into a sock's gaping mouth.

"My laundry," he mumbles as I roll off the bed and move to sit on the floor.

Donny shoves the clothes off his bed as I stare at a tear in his mattress and wonder if I even needed to look at a synastry chart. Shouldn't I have just read the *actual* signs of Richard's indifference to me? Wouldn't that have told me what I needed to know years ago? Were the stars deluding me or was I deluding myself?

Uncertainty ringing within me, I climb back on the bed and hand Donny my script.

Donny has been helping me learn my lines. The play is about two couples, one younger and one older, whose reservations for a weekend getaway cabin were double-booked. The play is written like a sitcom, was probably funnier twenty years ago, and moves entirely through one-liners where the punchlines belong almost entirely to the husband of the older couple, who also happens to be the director.

"Peggy says, 'Frank had a Republican upbringing. Nobody apologizes for anything,'" Donny says, giving me the cue.

"It's really delicious champagne. Tony doesn't like it that much, but he buys it for me. I love it. And I love him too! You fabulous, great-looking person!"

"Okay, that's right. Now, Frank's line, 'It's new. Somebody's gotta try it.'"

"You'd better bring in some more bottles of champagne. Let's make this a night to remember!"

Donny looks at me and grimaces.

I grimace back. It's terrible. It's really terrible.

Next scene.

"Frank says, 'Too bad. It might be good for you once in a while.'"

"God, the beaches were pure white, weren't they Tony? And the water was crystal blue and the air! It was just unbelievable!"

Donny skips ahead.

"Alright, now, let's go random."

He closes the script, flips it around, upside down, and sideways, and opens it to a random page.

"Okay. Here's Tony's line, 'You're getting your period, right? You always talk crazy a couple of days before you have your period. Thank God you're getting your period, for a while I thought . . . '"

His face turns to disgust.

"Who the fuck says things like this? This is bullshit. *Nobody* actually fucking talks this way."

Later that night, as I put the astrological textbooks I had consulted to determine my compatibility with Richard back on my bookshelf, I thought about the lines we say to one another, about our attempts to put bewilderment or sorrow into words, to answer how or why.

I thought about our gaping silences.

So who says stuff like this? Like lines in a sitcom? Like the sentences that you never thought you would find yourself saying or not saying across from people you never thought you'd say them to? Like the words we say because there's nothing else to say?

We do.

Fish

Your Reading For: February 14, 2013
It's on the end cap. It's always been there. Write
down what you need—do not be so arrogant, little
Ram, as to assume that you will always remember.

A dozen red roses stand lovely and oblivious on the dining room table before my mother and Bruce. She slumps against the chair, her hair greasy and matted, lipstick misplaced on her mouth. A plate of steak and baby red potatoes remain untouched and growing cold as she limply unwraps a heart-shaped chocolate praline in her lap.

Bruce sets a cellophane-wrapped box tied with a red ribbon before her.

Happy Valentine's Day, baby.

Hands trembling, she reaches for the gift. She unties the ribbon and watches the cellophane unfold.

It's a box.

A pink, metallic box.

She stares at Bruce.

He grabs the box, rips the top off, and turns it upside down. A perfume bottle shimmies out. He sets the bottle on the table as the overhead light illuminates the prismatic cap.

She stares at it.

The perfume seizes her.

This is not a test-tube sized bottle or something meant to last for six months of squirts or even made to last a year. This bottle is a joke, an impossible delusion, a gift in ignorance of the truth. And she knows it.

93

Bruce hands her a card and kisses her lips. As she turns away to shove her thumb under the envelope's seal, her eyes transfix on that bottle with enough fragrance to last if she made it to sixty.

Downstairs, I drag Donny into the bathroom and ask him for a favor.

"Sniff it?"

"Yeah, I mean, tell me what it smells like to you in here," I ask, leaning against the sink.

He closes his eyes and breathes in.

"It smells like fish . . . and flowers. Fish and flowers."

His eyes spring open.

"Courtney. Why does it smell like *fish* in here?"

He glares at me. I squirm.

"Courtney. Why does it *smell* like *fish*—"

I readjust myself against the sink, trying to look casual and unperturbed by my greasy torso, unfazed by the shimmering floor, unalarmed by the overwhelming smell of gill-bearing aquatic animals radiating from this bathroom. I cross my arms. I try to look confident. I try not to breathe.

"I was doing something with cod liver oil."

"*Cod liver oil?* What the fuck were you doing with *cod liver oil?*"

"Well . . . it was supposed to be castor oil and then I got confused when I went to the store and bought cod liver oil instead."

"Why are you buying all these *oils?*"

I stand up straight, propelling myself from the sink.

"They're for my lady parts."

"Your *lady* parts? Good *God*. I don't wanna fuckin' know—"

"Actually! Donny! Maybe you *do* want to know! Maybe you *should* know, Mr. Recently-Had-An-Ulcer-And-Gets-Lots-of-Headaches! You wanna know why? Because sadness has burrowed itself in my uterus and it hurts! I can feel our grief and it has manifested itself my right ovary!"

Donny's mouth hangs slack. I've already told him I bought cod liver oil. I've already started a rant about energy healing. The floor is already grimy and air is already stinky.

So I tell him everything.

"Donny, our thoughts *embed* themselves in our *bodies*! Our feelings *matter*! They *influence* us. And too much negative stuff means *pain*. And I read that if I smeared castor oil on myself, I could clear up the pain. Well, okay, my plan wasn't to *smear* it. You're supposed to make a pack or something and put it on your belly and let it sit there for a while. So I was going to do that but I bought the wrong oil. But I thought I should try it anyway. But, you know, I didn't think it would come out of the bottle so fast and while I was on the bathroom floor trying to put it on myself it kind of went everywhere. Like on the floor and rug and everything. So I had to mop it up and I sprayed some stuff to help cover up the smell. So there! Now you know. And now . . . you should go get some castor oil too."

Donny gawks at me.

"You're nuts. You're completely nuts. You and what's-his-nuts, *Richard* or whoever, really are meant for one another. You're both fuckin' weird."

He stalks off to his bedroom and slams the door.

I turn back to the bathroom, smear my thumb against the floor, and hold it up. It glistens with oil.

I flip the bathroom fan on, listen to it churn, and go upstairs.

Bruce covers my mother's dinner in plastic wrap at the counter while she sits at the table.

I walk over to the table and plop in Bruce's seat.

"What did you get?" I ask.

"Perfume," she whispers, turning the bottle to face me.

"Can I hold it?"

She nods her head yes, and I grab the bottle. It looks like a flask.

"It's really pretty."

I lift my shirt up and spritz the perfume on my belly.

Her face cracks into a smirk.

I pull my shirt up around my bra, spray my gut twice more, and drag my chair closer to her.

"Wha'does it smell like?" I ask.

She presses her nose against my belly button, confusion sprouting across her face.

"Fish?"

Virginia's Closet

Your Reading For: February 15, 2013
   When you become so narrow-minded, focused on achieving one desire, you may miss out on other opportunities. Take each experience on its own terms. Relish what you still have, little Ram.

I already know the lines for my other job back at the hotel, back in my black polyester, answering the phones, booking reservations, tearing the copy machine apart, and stocking the coffee bar.

Besides the corporate gains from an increased demand for Kleenex and booze, grief is not a productive endeavor in the professional sense. On a résumé, it's the void you will continually explain. Or you are the perpetual workplace autopsy. Hearing the wrong song or seeing a stranger with the same earrings as my mother would make me feel as though I was gutted, sliced from skull to shins in a breath. My agony exposed for all to see—I'd feel as though I was falling apart.

This time, it's Barry Manilow's "Can't Smile Without You" trickling through the radio while I'm counting the cash register at the end of the afternoon shift. I heart that whistle, that delicate piano, and my guts begin to quiver. I know what's coming. I try to focus on counting the change. I start with the quarters and all the while that sappy voice streams through the radio and by now I've cried so much that it's an autonomous function, a nearly unconscious response. I go to the dimes and the whistling is back— the urge to weep looms wide. I go to the nickels and that *voice*— so *melodramatic*—and all my sorrow is Barry Manilow's sorrow and his sorrow is mine and then it happens—crying. I'm flat-out blubbering, xiphoid escaped, wet and pulsing on the desk, lungs heaving behind. I stand up and it feels as though all of my insides, blood and bile and mucus, career down my legs and splatter at my feet.

Yes. This is routine—even the gasp escaping from my mouth.

The head housekeeper mutters behind the copy machine in the back room, "What's wrong with her?"

"Her mother is really sick. Like, *dying.*"

And that is the sideshow performance. Where you are roadkill, twitching and writhing on the highway, your profound misery blown open from the inside out, sprayed across the pavement for everyone to drive past, stare at, and continue on with their lives.

I leave the desk and wander into the bathroom.

Once there, I gaze into the mirror. Mascara runs down my face, concealer blotchy on my shirt collar.

Someone's knocking on the door.

"Justa minute."

I blow my nose, smear my face on a paper towel, open the door, and prepare to take my bow.

Back at the desk, once my boss and the head housekeeper meander to the kitchen to get a slice of pie, I lean back in my chair and stare across the empty hotel lobby.

The Christmas decorations are still up around the lobby's perimeter; they all move. The Santa dances, the Angels' wings flap, and a Snowman boogies. Their motors and joints creak back and forth. I can hear the building manager scraping the sidewalk outside, his shovel smacking and screeching against the concrete. I look at the clock behind me. An hour until I'm done. A centipede crawls up the wall and disappears behind the clock. I'm supposed to be sorting reservations and highlighting credit card numbers and dusting the computer keyboard.

I call my mother from the hotel phone.

She picks up and answers with a faint hello.

"Mom? Do you want to break into Tom's house after my shift?"

She pauses.

"We can drink his booze," I say, assuming she'd never say yes, assuming she knows I'm joking, assuming she knows I'm calling because I'm bored at work.

"Sure," she whispers.

It's not really breaking in. I have a key. I'm supposed to check in on my father's dogs while he and his wife are gone for the day. I pick my mother up and we go over to his house.

Snow piled mountainous on either side of his driveway, we shuffle up to the door. I turn the lock and peer inside. The Labradors' snouts are pressed to the crack, wet noses stacked one by one, sniffing and shaking. The simultaneous funk of unwashed fur, wet leather boots, and charred venison from last night's dinner seeps through the opening. I swing the door open and the dogs charge us, dancing and wiggling, tails wagging. My mother stands back silent and withered. I help her to the couch and she sinks into it. The dogs swarm her, sniffing, licking, rooting at her hands for her to pet them. She taps their heads while I pour food into their bowls and they bolt.

"Do you really want some wine?" I ask, sitting next to her on the couch.

She looks at me, her face a frown.

"No." She stares at the floor. "I'm not supposed to drink."

One of the dogs comes back and roots at my hand for me to pet her. I scratch her chin.

"Let's look in Virginia's closet," my mother whispers.

The other dogs come over and root at my other hand.

". . . You wanna look in Virginia's closet?" I ask.

"Yeah."

". . . Okay," I reply.

We creep upstairs into their bedroom. Muddy dog and boot prints dot the alabaster carpeting. Pictures of Tom and Virginia on their wedding day hang on one wall. Crooked prints of ducks flying over marshes populate the others; my father's electric boot dryer stands tall in the corner.

I slide Virginia's closet doors open. The wood-paneled closet is haphazardly stuffed, a bouquet of fabrics, price tags, and shoeboxes spilling onto the floor and packed to the ceiling. My mother picks up a straw hat with a wide, dramatic brim and puts it on. She pulls out a salmon-colored sarong and wraps it around herself. She digs through the fabrics and finds a faux-leather jacket. I stand astonished—that she came with me, that she's here, that she wanted to look in Virginia's closet. She puts the leather jacket on and glides over to their bed where she leans back and lets herself fall onto the mattress, arms stretched out as though she were making a snow angel, hat crushed underneath her head.

My mother closes her eyes as the gentle curve of a smile settles across her face and I wonder what fantasy she dwells in, what floats through her mind as she's sprawled across her ex-husband's bed in his wife's clothing.

The dogs start to shuffle below us—their nails click, they whine and yip.

An engine bellows. The garage door churns.

My mother looks at me and whispers, "Tom . . ."

She pulls herself upright, shimmies out of the jacket, whips the sarong off, and holds the clothing out to me. I grab and throw it all back into the closet, slamming the doors shut. When I turn around, my mother is still perched on the edge of the bed grinning, watching me scurry around.

"Mom—"

She giggles. She throws her hand over her mouth and laughs, her chest shuddering.

"Mom—we have to *go*. She'll be so pissed if she knows we were looking through her *stuff*. . ."

And we move, as quickly as we can, back down the stairs where we run right into my father standing in the kitchen.

We freeze.

My father looks at me, his blue eyes expressionless.

"Uh. Hi, Dad. Mom just came with me to watch the dogs. We were . . . looking around . . . upstairs."

"Oh. We got back early," he says, sitting on a kitchen stool, seemingly unfazed.

"Oh yeah?" I ask, nervous.

My father pieces through the mail collecting on the kitchen table—a letter from AARP, a postcard from State Farm Insurance, a sporting goods magazine . . .

"Yeah—Carl. Carl's in the hospital. We have to go over there. It's, ah, pretty bad this time."

Carl is my ninety-six-year-old grandfather.

Virginia is in the living room, cooing at the dogs.

"Is this . . . it?" I whisper.

My father wipes his nose against his sleeve.

"I don't know, Cork."

". . . Did he ask for a hot beef?"

"No. Not this time. He's, you know, pretty sick," he replies.

We all stare at the floor.

Does my father not find this strange that his ex-wife is standing in his kitchen? Is this all normal to him? Or is he too stunned by his father's impending death to ask? Why did *I* bring my mother over here and put her in this?

My mother grabs my hand and squeezes it.

"Dad, I think Mom and I should go—you know, the roads. I'll—I'll call you later."

We start toward the door when my father touches my mother's shoulder.

She stops and turns around.

He opens his arms to her.

I stop.

She cocks her head. I hold my breath.

His face goes slack and she shuffles into his arms.

Murmuring, he holds her and I watch as she leaks onto his fishing shirt, all of us suspended, all of us held, until Virginia's feet shuffle toward the kitchen and they pull apart.

I take my mother's hand and we flee to the car.

Linking arms to stay upright, we inch across the icy walk as a discarded orange peel, nearly fluorescent against the snow, sits forgotten beside the driveway.

Triple Pit

Your Reading For: February 16, 2013

Young Aries! Now is your chance—tears cannot talk. They will not betray you. They are not colored different shades that correspond with why they are cried. Though you risk misinterpretation, weep away.

Carl believed he was dying his entire life. Family trips were canceled, prescriptions were collected en masse, days were spent in bed with the covers pulled up to his nostrils on the brink of the end. There's a picture of my father as a little boy holding a birthday cake next to his father in bed. All you see are Carl's eyes peeking out from behind the blanket. According to my father, "That was my eighth birthday and the seventy-fourth time Carl was dying."

My father told us of having to follow him to work every day because Carl feared he would perish on the way to work either by crashing his car or by somehow dying in a way unrelated to the car and then unconsciously crashing his car. He told us about the suspect members of the medicine chest, stuff like "the pink juice" that Carl took to ease his near-annihilation anxieties; it was an opium product that was eventually recalled. Carl once went to the Packerland meat plant, purchased a steer gallbladder, boiled it, and then drank the goop—another remedy for his "my death is imminent" dread. Multiple times he was given final meals on his deathbed at various hospitals. A hot beef? You got it. A banana split? Lemme get that for you! A box of powdered donut holes? I'll get two!

And, each time, he lived!

Donny takes a sip of gin and something and looks pained. Sitting in the basement, we are back in The Pit. This time, I am playing therapist. This time, it's Extreme Pit. The stinkiest of the stink. The Pittiest of The Pit sessions. There are new elements involved. No longer are we simply processing, this is Triple Pit. Add heartbreak, add rejection. It's 2 a.m. and the devastation started hours ago.

Donny's ranting.

"You know, sometimes. No, always—EVERY. SINGLE. THING. SUCKS. I'm sitting here DOING NOTHING. I'm un-FUCKING-employed. My girlfriend is off with somebody else. I got cut from the team. And! AND Mom is DYING. I wake up every day and think 'Okay, what's next? What's the next thing that's going to go wrong?'"

The following morning we receive a phone call. Carl died last night.

He drifted away while dreaming, the day after our late grand-mother's birthday. *Happy Birthday, baby.* I envision them nestled inside a rainbow somewhere, sharing a belated angel food cake covered in stardust.

I am the only one who cries at his funeral. Everything is too topical. We'd wandered into a Dali painting, some surrealist waste-land where the message written in the sand with a finger says, *Keep That Black Dress Handy!*

After the service, we all filter back into the funeral home lobby. There's decaf coffee and cake along one wall and everyone is wearing a different brand of cologne and perfume. Between that and the flowers, the air feels thick enough to grab. I grab a styro-foam cup of decaf as my eyes dart from flower arrangement to flower arrangement to the giant photograph of Carl smiling at seventy-two, his dentures shiny and new, his thin comb-over per-fectly coiffed. Behind me, my father talks to his second cousins while Donny eats dinner mint after dinner mint from the candy bowl by the lobby door. I stare at the laminated photo of my grandfather and think that if I could see Carl again I'd ask him, was dying really the fun part? Did you time this to mock your grandchildren? Your final comedic death wish? Not donut holes but searing irony? Not banana splits but black comedy?

Or has Carl actually given us a practice run? A view into the future—*See these flower arrangements? That schmaltzy picture? The swarming relatives? Get ready!*

I spot Donny out of the corner of my eye. He grabs a handful of dinner mints, shoves them in his pocket, meanders from the candy dish to a flower arrangement. He sticks his face in an Easter lily, breathes in, and sneezes into the flower. He pulls his face out bewildered and sniffling.

Donny rubs his hand against his nose and jiggles the mints around in his pocket with the other and walks up to me. I reach out my hand to touch the portrait of Carl and lay it against his two-dimensional shoulder, the painting leatherlike against my hand.

"Court, do you wanna dinner mint? I gotta bunch," Donny whispers behind me.

"I'm okay," I reply, still staring at our grandfather's glossy face. Donny shoves another mint into his mouth and crunches as I whisper, "Thank you, Carl. Thank you for our dress rehearsal."

Sing

Your Reading For: March 2, 2013
Yes, we get it—your ego is large and your sense of shame always looms, blah, blah. We've heard it before. Let it go, impetuous Ram. Accept life as it comes and turn up that radio!

Snow splatters against the windshield.

I flip the wipers on as my mother and I drive in silence to a doctor's appointment. We barrel along the wet roads, dry warmth shuddering through the vents. Her silence is no longer a choice but a symptom of her illness. Tumors have spread throughout her body, rolling hills of disease. One mound rests on her throat, constricting her vocal cords. Her voice sounds like a clementine's cry—something tiny and sweet, hidden behind a mealy peel.

The radio call sign ends and a clarinet coos.

A piano murmurs.

Karen Carpenter's voice, smooth and whole, streams through the speakers.

I know this song.

She's singing about optimism and hope.

She's "only just begun."

I am captured.

Richard Carpenter joins her and I fume, my hands nearly strangling the steering wheel.

I should change the station. This is not *easy* listening. This song is *mocking* us. This is not what we need to hear. We need Donna Summer singing about bad girls and disco. We need the Bee Gees singing about nights on Broadway. We need a soundtrack of distraction. We should be listening to talk radio or to the weather report or the sound of our own meditative breathing or nothing at all.

I take a hand off the wheel to turn the dial when my mother inhales and wheezes along to the backing vocals—Richard Carpenter's part.

I keep driving and the song keeps going and I swear I might bifurcate right here and now in this driver's seat. The heater blows hot against my face; I can feel myself start to sweat.

She pats my arm to join in.

. . . *She wants me to sing this?*

The song drones on and she keeps tapping my arm.

I glare at the road.

She grabs my arm and shakes it.

She whispers my name and starts singing Karen's lyrics.

I glare at the stop signal. I glare at the sidewalk. I glare at the hospital in the distance.

I inhale and I sing, nearly choking on the lyrics.

I flick my blinker on to turn into the hospital entrance and idle until the song finishes, the four of us sing the final lyrics together—Richard, Karen, my mother, and me.

My mother unbuckles her seatbelt and wordlessly climbs out of the car. A hospital volunteer greets her with a wheelchair and I watch them go through the sliding glass doors. As she disappears into the lobby, I close my eyes and collapse against the steering wheel. Have we only just begun? Or is this the ending of our relationship? I turn my head to watch her disappear down the hospital corridor, car rumbling, and wonder if this is a moment of hope—*we sang the song together!* Or if this is a moment of cruel irony—*we sang the song together!*

The next morning my mother and I sit down at the dinner table to sort through her sympathy cards. She asked me to buy "Thank You" notes for her responses and I told her I would help her by addressing the envelopes and licking them shut.

I hand her the cards and a pen.

My mother's treatment involves focusing a beam of radiation at the crown of her head. The radiation has warped her hair follicles and given her a new Friar Tuck hairstyle. With her back to the lakeside window, she sits against the stark white background: a snow-covered beach, frozen lake, and stoic sky. She is a living piece of Delftware. Blue veins run in delicate spindles against her bald scalp.

Sitting across from her, I numb myself by being efficient: licking stamps, writing return addresses, and slapping the envelopes in a pile. Minutes pass before I realize that my mother hasn't moved.

A single card spreads vacant before her. The pen purposeless like a prop.

". . . Mom?"

"I don't know what to say," she whispers.

She looks at me, her eyes searching.

"What do I tell them?"

I shift in my seat.

"What do I write, Courtney? I . . ."

Her eyes dart from the pile of cards to the pile of blank notes and back.

"I can tell you what to write, Mom."

". . . Yeah?"

"Yeah. I'll—I'll tell you what to say. We'll just go through the cards one by one . . ."

". . . Okay."

She poises her pen, eyes steady on mine.

I turn to the pile of cards and after reading them aloud to her, I dictate the responses:

> Dear retired coworker/lady she went to high school with/ex-boyfriend/etc.,
>
> Thank you so much for your card and the gift certificate to Red Lobster. I appreciate you thinking of me and my family. Your friendship has meant so much to me. I've missed seeing you at work/in the post-op room/at Poo's/at bingo/at poker, but I don't miss how you always took my money (ha!). I hope you have a wonderful time on your trip to Jamaica/your daughter's ballet recital goes well/your son's hockey games are fun/you can make it through the hospital's construction on the third floor. Have a good winter and stay warm!
>
> Love,
> Vicky

Card after card; after Dear Ronnie, after Dear Roberta, after Dear Shannon; after have fun in Florida, have fun in Cancún, good luck at bingo; I peel off the stamps and seal the envelopes while my mother shuffles to the couch to watch the afternoon news report.

I take the cards to the mailbox.

Snow swirls as I lift the red flag and shut the metal box. As I turn around to walk home, I wonder if she will ever write back to me. I wonder what she would say.

Freaks

Your Reading For: March 17, 2013
Oh Aries, it is difficult to give but one piece of advice that will work for all situations so, today, let us give you two. One—pass no judgment and say no thing. Two—judge away and let yourself be heard.

Welcome to Poo's.
Today, this fishing tavern swarms with green beer-drinking, emerald-teethed St. Patrick's day partiers, packed wall to wall, yelling and inebriated, wearing plastic leprechaun hats, with AC/DC's "Back in Black" booming above the crowd.

We're here for the slots. We're here for a beer. We're here because my family just watched a matinee showing of the play at the dinner theater. We're here to help my mother move to the back of the bar with Donny on one side and Bruce on the other. Paige, Donny's girlfriend, and I trail behind. Our mother sets the pace and that means we move slowly. As we crawl to the back of the bar, I watch clusters of loud, yelping conversations turn to whispers about the skeletal woman drifting through the bar with her entourage. Their eyes ogle her slow gait, her saggy jeans, her hollow face—*Doesn't she look like that lady who used to come here all the time?*

With each step, I convince myself she's thinking about something else—the music, the neon craft brewery signs, how Bruce's hand feels in hers. I convince myself that she wouldn't care anyway. I convince myself to smile and focus on our destination and sanctuary: the slot machines.

Once there, we steer my mother to a machine and I give her all the change in my purse. Bruce and Donny push their way to the bar to get a drink while Paige and I sit next to my mother on high-top black leather bar stools, where we twist back and forth like windshield wipers. Paige takes her program out of her back pocket and flips through it.

Paige is visiting Donny from Oklahoma and staying with us in the basement. The only details I know were derived from pressing my ear to Donny's bedroom door, but they've apparently worked out their "issues" and are together again, much to Donny's glee. Paige is basically a younger version of our mother with a sluggish Southern drawl and an affinity for body piercings and tattoos. Paige can slam shots and drink Long Island Ice Teas and walk out of the bar in a straight line. She smokes cigarettes on the back porch with Bruce, holding the cigarette between her pointer and middle finger in a way that makes me wish I smoked. She draws complex lines in liquid eyeliner along her brown eyes, paints on a pouty red mouth with lipstick after smoking, and changes her hair color monthly. Right now, she's a pageant girl blonde with Farrah Fawcett curls. Paige studied nursing, like our mother, before dropping out of the program to, ironically, study mortuary science. She's the only person I've met from Oklahoma and based on her I assume everyone from Oklahoma is someone I'd want as my sister or cousin or aunt—a woman you have on standby to rant with and watch drink more than you thought was possible for a body that clocks in just over five feet. I love her just as much as Donny does.

"HE *DOES* LOOK AT YOUR CROTCH ON THAT LINE," Paige says to me, her mouth against my ear, referring to the line where Richard's character says that the reason my character is acting "crazy" is because I have my period.

"I KNOW. IT'S REALLY WEIRD."

Richard always looks at the front of my jeans as though there were a green light or sign that hangs off your fly during menstruation. I thought it was strange. I'd told Paige to look for it.

We turn our attention to my mother and watch the reels turn. They spin to a stop. No win. Credits disappear. *Play Again!* Paige and I gasp audibly like a sitcom audio track. My mother shoves more quarters into the machine, her face withered into a frown. She glances at us and, realizing that we're watching her, flashes us a faint grin.

Everyone's an actor today.

Bruce and Donny return from the bar and hand a drink to each of us. My mother and I each get a glass of water with a lemon in it; everyone else gets a beer. Donny leans over.

"IDIDUNHTKNOWHUTUUUWHANND."

"What?"

"IJUSSSGOTUUWHADDER. IDIDUNHTKNOWHUTUUUWHANND."

I take a sip of the water to indicate that, yes, it's all I wanted. Bruce puts his arm around my mother and watches the reels revolve.

Paige shoves her face into my ear and says, "I CAN'T HEAR ANYTHING IN HERE."

"I CAN'T EITHER."

The three of us swing on bar stools and watch the crowd. We watch hands slip around unfamiliar waists and mockingly "whip the bird" as punctuation to stories and caress the wood paneled walls for support as people stumble to and from the bathroom. We watch beers slammed on the bar and drinks left on stools to be forgotten and booze spilt down shirts. The squeal of a Poison solo ricochets through our chests and we make our way through Bon Jovi and Metallica on the jukebox until Donny finishes the last third of his beer in one gulp and suggests we get the hell out of here.

While Donny, Bruce, and Paige assemble around our mother to lead her out of the bar, I lag behind and watch the same clusters of whispers ripple through the bar about my mother while a middle-aged man with a thin gray crewcut, potbelly, and a face like a bulldog leans against the bar holding a plastic cup of green beer.

I watch him stare at my mother and look her entourage up and down. I watch him shout to the bartender, "You shouldn't let a bunch of *freaks* into your bar—it's bad for business."

He laughs.

I stop.

He keeps laughing, belly heaving, smiling his green-toothed smile as he turns to watch my family leave through the screen door and take a swig of his green beer and I want to punch him. I want to get right up in his green-toothed, sweaty, red face and tell him, That woman? That sick *freak*? She's dying. And this is the last time she'll ever set foot in this bar. This is the last time she'll ever sit on a leather-top bar stool and watch her credits disappear. This is the last time she'll travel a hundred yards without a walker or a wheelchair. This is the last everything. *And that makes you a complete prick.*

I imagine slapping him, that feeling of his stubbly face in my palm, turning my drink upside down in his crotch, watching the liquid splatter and spread, rage foaming and manifesting in the saliva I spit in his face. I imagine the delicious way his face would crinkle and grimace as my spit would hit him. I imagine spinning on my heel, listening to the door slap behind me, and sprinting into the parking lot.

Instead, I give him my best expressionless *read my subtext, asshole*, midwestern stare as I walk away and out of the bar.

I catch up to everyone else at the car where Donny holds the door open for me. He grins.

"What?" I snap.

"Takin' that with you?" He gestures toward my left hand.

I clutch an empty water glass with melted ice, a squeezed lemon rolling around the bottom. I never put it back on the bar.

I slide into the backseat.

"Yes, Donny. I'm taking it with me."

At two o'clock that night I awake to thunder.

I inch up the stairs until I can see across the kitchen floor—it's Bruce sprawled out, riding the wood floor's stagnant wave in his bathrobe. A half empty Maker's Mark whisky bottle keeps watch from the countertop.

He keeps trying to stand.

And he keeps falling.

I run down the stairs and into Donny's room and jerk his shoulder around to wake him up, "It's *Bruce.*"

"What?"

"It's *Bruce.* He's up there flailing around. He can't stand."

The rumble of Bruce's fall reverberates above us.

"Christ," Donny hisses and hops out of bed.

We both go up the stairs and stop at eye level to watch him. Bruce has moved about three inches from where I first saw him five minutes ago.

"Go help him, Donny!" I hiss.

Donny stomps up to the kitchen, pulls Bruce to his feet, and maneuvers him to the couch. Donny sits in an armchair, I stand on the stairs, and we both wait for Bruce to pass out as the furnace clunks and moans beneath us.

Bruce falls asleep.

Donny rests his head back on the armchair.

I crouch on the steps, the floor cold on my bare feet.

Once they are both wheezing, I go back downstairs and crawl into bed.

Burrowing into my pillow, I see the pile of horoscope clippings sitting on the nightstand beside me. I look at them and think of the man at the bar. His green teeth. My mother's frown. Her fabricated smile. Richard knowingly looking at my crotch. Shame washing over me. The questions clamoring within me. *Rewind, repeat.* That little crewcut. Potbelly wrapped underneath his shirt. What if I asked her? *Freaks.* My mother shuffling. People whispering. Richard's perfunctory, cold hand in mine during the curtain call. Black out. *Rewind, repeat . . .*

Hours later, I hear Bruce's feet plod to the counter. The coffee maker gurgles. I hear the front door slam; he's off to work. As I stare out of my bedroom window at the morning haze, I wonder how he's able to perform again each day. I finally drift to sleep, *How else can I kno*—my final conscious thought.

Prayer Blanket

Your Reading For: April 2, 2013
This Place of silence and doubt is certainly found
in your hometown, but there's a reason you haven't
been calling "This Place" Prairie du Chien or Jim
Falls or the physical location you're actually from.
Because "This Place" you've described can be
found anywhere.

My mother lounges, hair turban-clad, a glass of lambic raspberry beer in her hand, a novel fanned facedown at her side. Snow blows off the roof and scatters as the television revolves between coverage of the Jodi Arias trial and Italy overturning Amanda Knox's acquittal. Her slippered feet rest on the table, a freshly laundered robe tied at her waist, and if you were to spot her without context—if you could see us as strangers through the window—this person on the couch could be perfectly content, a woman relaxing on her day off, a woman sampling stories and foreign booze at eleven a.m.

Spot me without context and you'll see a sleep-deprived young woman sitting at the kitchen table behind my mother. You'll see a woman already anxious within minutes of waking, a woman with newspaper clippings clammy between her hands that she places face-up one by one. You'll see her skimming the clippings, her mouth twisting, glancing at the woman on the couch. You'll see a daughter analyzing the evidence and coming to the conclusion that has pressed against her for weeks but she could not bear to face. Final analysis: she can no longer avoid the questions that badger her. They have grown more urgent, each a second closer to the regret of never asking.

Without context, you'll see me walking toward the woman on the couch. It is then you realize that the woman on the couch is ill—her skin unnaturally yellow, her cheeks sunken. That relaxed ease was an illusion; the woman on the couch casually slumps because she cannot hold herself up. If you were to wonder what runs through the ill woman's mind, your speculations would be echoed by those who surround her. Does she wonder if her previous choices have manifested in her illness? Does anger bubble and rust over inside of her? Does she plot ways to short-circuit her inevitable end? Does she think of the cosmic rationale for her death? Does she ask *why me*?

The daughter who sits down on the couch next to her has contemplated the same questions. She collapses within seconds onto her mother's frail lap, pulled down by an overwhelming apprehension about how to chart the unknown, about how to live without her axis point—her mother. You'll see that daughter sit upright to show her mother the newspaper clippings—not as evidence of the universe's guidance but as evidence of the daughter's desperation, her stupidity, her naïveté. You'll see that young woman heave and weep. You'll see a daughter despondent, asking her mother for confirmation of her belief, promise of their continued connection, acknowledgment of their impending separation. You'll see her purge the questions she has carried with her for months and that, perhaps, she should've purged months ago.

You'll see the woman on the couch look through the clippings and turn her eyes back to the television coverage. You'll see her drink the rest of her beer in one gulp. And you'll see that woman look her daughter in the eye. She shakes her head. She tells her daughter that she just . . . just can't believe in much of anything anymore.

And you'll see that daughter nod and say that she understands.

And if you were a stranger standing in the snow as you watch us turn back to the television, you'll see shock spreading through me as I realize that I had led myself to believe that if I waited long enough, if I could only gather my desperation up and present it to her, if I could be selfish enough to even ask, maybe she would say yes.

Hours later it's all frivolity. Impending death of an estranged relative? It's time to brunch! Somehow the news must've traveled. *The end is near! Final showing! Last call!* And mysterious family members from the far reaches of Minnesota and Milwaukee have arrived on our doorstep carrying coffee cake, clam chowder, and Epsom salts. I shut the television off and make a pot of coffee, Bruce shuffles the woman of the hour to the dinner table and plops her in a chair while Donny sprints to his car and drives the twenty miles to our father's house to escape.

Enter relatives.

It's hats and scarves off. It's hand the clam chowder to Bruce and the Epsom salts to me. It's "Where's Vicky?" and hushed voices. It's tissues in the corners of eyes at the sight of her. It's me pouring coffee. It's Bruce slicing up the coffee cake. It's them huddling around my mother. It's a distant cousin pulling out a blanket with a bow and handing it to my mother. It's my mother's astonishment at this silk woven blanket with a pouch. It's silence as my mother stares at it and reads the corresponding instruction card. It's the cousin whispering to my mother, "It's a prayer blanket, Vicky."

And then my mother looks to me.

And it's her face staring directly at me holding this prayer blanket. It's the face of *What the hell are we doing here?* Here, in this kitchen surrounded by these near-stranger relatives who've driven hours to see her, aroused only by her teetering on the edge of death, in This Place where we chatter about the weather and coffee cake and avoid discussing both the literal and figurative elephants in the room. In this situation where people are handing her prayer blankets so that she will write her dreams and fears and shove them into the blanket's pocket with the hope that they will materialize . . . when it is plainly obvious there's nothing she could hope for or do or say that would make any difference. And it's me, holding the coffee carafe, feeling as though the floor is bottoming out beneath me and I completely understand her sentiment and I nearly speak it with the subtext emanating from my mother's gaping mouth, *What are we doing here?* How could we have ever believed that anything in the Deep End could guide us? How could I ever ask her to send me *messages?* How could I ask her to be on the other end? How could I ask her to believe? How and why am *I* believing? And how could she put a prayer in this blanket?

She can't manage it. And she won't.

And so my mother takes that scarf, and with those bamboo arms, thinner than I thought possible, wraps that blanket around her head like a hood. And she grins, making eye contact with each person at that table. And we are silent, stunned, uncertain. And I put the carafe on the table and bust out laughing. I bowl over onto the table, resting on elbows, face in hands, and laugh and laugh and then it's me bawling. Me bawling on the kitchen table while my mother wears a prayer blanket and a bunch of near-strangers stare at me.

And someone laughs.

And then they all laugh. They roar. And it's me sobbing. Sobbing on the table. And it's my mother taking the blanket off her head and letting it gather around her shoulders. It's her saying thank you. Thank you for the prayer blanket. And it's me sobbing. Sobbing next to the coffee cake. And it's me standing up, telling everybody I'm taking the Epsom salts to their new home, I'm taking them to the bathroom. I grab them by their handle and stumble to my mother's bathroom.

And once there I flip the fan on, toss the Epsom salts into the tub, crawl in there with them, press a towel over my face, and howl.

Somehow, even though my Deep End confidant—my mother—was dying, I had felt all along that it would become clear that she wouldn't be gone forever. I was waiting for confirmation. We splashed around in the Deep End! And now my mother was going into the ultimate Deep End, so shouldn't she be there with me as well? Shouldn't death not matter in this? I had clung harder to the divinatory methods I knew because I thought, believed, that my mother would still be on the other end. That I could tap that cosmic phone line, twirl my fingers around the cord, and listen to her messages blaring from the other end. I believed that my mother would be there, waiting for me, talking to me despite her physical absence.

I wanted to believe.

I lift the towel off my face and try to breathe.

But how could she even think of that now? How could she believe in some saving grace of the afterlife when her life is cut short? How could I be so foolish as to believe that she would be there waiting for me, talking to me when she wasn't even talking to anyone on earth? How could I be so ignorant as to think that clinging to rocks, tarot cards, or astrological predictions could save me, swaddle me from the reality of my mother's absence? That man years ago at the bar was right, my mother and father both spoke of her death, my clothing fell apart, but what did it matter? What did it matter if esoteric predictions happened? They still happen. What was the point of anything I invested faith in?

I smear my face in my sweater and flip onto my side, holding the bath salt bag like a teddy bear. I stare into the fiberglass siding. In the dry womb of this tub, I am alone. And it is my choice to flip the faucet on and bathe in faith—faith that this would mean something, faith that she will be there on the other side, faith in rocks and cards and smoke—or to lie dry. Do I continue to believe?

Laughter echoes from the dining room. I hug the Epsom salt closer, the plastic bag crinkling beneath my grip. They're talking about pontoons and invasive carp species and I realize even as I lie here, awash in doubt, I am still holding onto a bag of healing rocks.

Whatever . . . I flip to my opposite side, close my eyes, and listen for the hoarse tinkle of my mother's laugh among the dining-room conversation.

And when I cannot hear her, it's me climbing out of the tub, placing the salts on the floor, and walking back into the dining room where it's all chatter about Lake Michigan and Bruce making more coffee and my mother's gaunt fingers running across the surface of that prayer blanket. And it's my mother's thin face staring at me and me staring at her and it's her sliding her hand into the pocket where you can put handwritten prayers. And it's her hand staying inside that little prayer pocket and her staring right at me and me staring back at her. And it's Bruce's conversation with the cousin from Duluth about treatments in Switzerland, about doctors in Rochester, about possibly having five more years left, about new innovations in brain treatment and lymph regeneration. And it's my mother, the only one who can bear to look at the next bleak vista, as she silently pats her hand inside that prayer pocket like a heartbeat. *Bump bump . . . Bump bump . . .* And it's her grinning at me despite all of it, the absurdity of this moment more clear to her than anyone else.

Commercials

Your Reading For: April 15, 2013
  Remember, young Ram, around heavy machinery,
trucks, and table saws, mental paralysis is danger-
ous. Around the dying, it is inevitable. Take your
numbness and forge on.

The television is our metronome and the center of our domestic galaxy. We keep time with the weather updates and repeating pharmaceutical ads every half-hour as my mother and I sit collapsed onto one another like burlap potato bags on the couch. The geography of my mother's illness is unknown to me—I don't know where her sickness dwells or how it makes her ache—but this morning, for whatever the reason, everything is hilarious to her. She is childlike, my new playmate. I tell her we must look like potato sacks tossed on the couch and she giggles. I make her take her pills and she rolls her eyes and looks at the pills and cracks herself up. I play with her floppy hands and make them clap and she thinks I'm a riot. The audience members sprinting at a chance to play *The Price Is Right* make her snort. We hear white pines snap outside under the weight of snow. We turn to watch a branch crash to the ground and we shriek. My mother starts to ask me, "Do you remember when . . ."

She stares at me. She forgot what she was asking me to remember.

And she laughs. And I laugh. And then we look at one another and it's even funnier and we're two potato sacks giggling and snorting on the couch. And then a new commercial plays—we hear a seagull squawk. We hear waves roll, crash, and recede. We hear what must be—*a beach . . .*

Our heads snap to watch.

It's an advertisement for a travel agency. A man and woman run hand-in-hand across the sand, silhouetted against a setting sun. The water looks so blue and the heat radiating off the sand looks so glorious and I feel my mother's hands seize up in my own. The couple turns to hug one another as her face buckles, her eyes wet and full. Palm trees sway and fade. The weather report returns. Tears overflow and I see what that commercial was really advertising: *This is everything you want but can never have.*

I watch her little face shimmer and I fantasize about all the ways I could destroy this television. Kick it down the lake bank and listen to it crunch with each roll. Light it on fire in the driveway and watch it burn. Drown it in flat soda and see it sizzle and grow sticky. My mother squeezes my hands tighter as the afternoon soap operas start. She whispers, "I need my room."

I wipe her cheeks with my sweatshirt sleeve and tell her that I'll take her.

After moving the wheelchair to her and taking her to bed, I sit next to her on the mattress and wrap my arms around her: my paper doll mother, fragile and thin.

She places paper hands around my waist.

Holding her, I memorize the feeling of her body against mine as I see my fortune for the foreseeable future day-by-day scroll through my mind: *numbness prevails, indifference presides, this deadened feeling will last, anesthetized again dear Aries,* and so on. I close my eyes, breathe in, and pretend my mother is plastic. She's concrete or limestone. I pretend that, somehow, she is exempt from pain.

I pretend we are going to be swimming in the Adriatic Sea together in just a few weeks—we're still going to take our trip. We have our bags packed. She bought a new swimming suit. *Three* new suits on sale. She's been going to the tanning salon every week and I've practicing my basic Croatian phrases. We talk on the phone about it and remind the other to bring sunscreen and I am delusional.

I hold her closer.

She is a single stalk of wheat bending beneath my hold.

Opening my eyes, I look down at the woman in my arms.

She is asleep.

Eileen

Your Reading For: April 24, 2013
    Young Aries, the logic is simple. If you don't
tell someone, how can you blame them for not
knowing?

While my mother dreams and Donny battles aliens with a controller and Bruce works with charts and electricity usage figures in a windowless office, I deem myself the official "carrier of goods," the person who will run your errand, shovel the driveway, get that casserole dish back to this person, or pick up this prescription at a moment's notice.

I feel incapable of much else.

I'm at the grocery store carrying two packages of adult diapers and an enema kit under one arm and a gallon of chocolate-vanilla-swirl ice cream under the other. An intercom advertisement announcing discount Easter candy radiates throughout the store before switching back to the local country station. The floor is shiny and squeaky, nearly empty at two in the afternoon. I'm ambling around the cereal aisle, trying to remember the other thing Bruce told me to buy, when I spot a woman I went to high school with pondering the organic cereals.

Eileen.

Like Tiffany from Budapest, she's beautiful in that midwestern way where beauty is a formula with variations and exponents depending on whether you're married, single, or divorced. Her computation reads: *blonde highlights and lowlights + sparkly engagement ring so large your friends speculate it's fake + bronzer on your eyelids + protein powder mix replacement for lunch + women's cut Packer jersey to accentuate time at gym = beauty.*

Eileen and I had been partners in our sophomore biology class when we dissected raw chicken thighs; the high school couldn't afford frogs or fetal pigs. I remember her being popular and pretty and cordial to me when trying to find a vein in the chicken flesh. She did most of the work while I stood behind her shoulder and gagged. We even shared relieved faces afterwards as we cleaned up our lab area.

In situations like this in This Place, my usual course of action is to turn the opposite direction and pretend I'd never seen my long-long adolescent acquaintance and continue on toward the pet food aisle to hide until said acquaintance was most likely in some other aisle or the checkout line or, hopefully, the parking lot. I never knew what to say. Well, I did—but I felt uncomfortable about saying "How are you," "I've missed you," and "We should get together" when you really know you'll never see this person again and had you really cared how they were doing you would've called or asked their mother about them when you saw her at the greenhouse last spring.

But Eileen's already spotted me. She's holding a box of some berry flaxseed granola. She seems genuinely excited to spot a long-lost adolescent acquaintance. She's waving. She's smiling. She's walking toward me.

I have to talk to her.

"Courtney?"

"Eileen?"

We meet each other near the oatmeal and share an awkward too-loose hug where only our collarbones touch and the conversation commences.

We exchange the "Haven't seen *you* in so long" and the "How long has it been?" and I start with the "How are you?" and she tells me that she's great. Just got engaged, working in a clinic after getting her nursing degree, loves being back in This Place after going away to school in Madison. And she asks the "How are you?" to me. And I tell her that I've been traveling—just had a layover in Barcelona!—I've been really lucky, been able to see so much, and I'm home for now. She grins and nods and I grin and nod back.

Then we go off script.

"Barcelona?!" She sighs. "I've *always* wanted to go there! You know, say, if I ever had something terrible, like, you know, *terminal cancer* or something I'd just take my family's credit cards and go traveling. I'd go to Spain and Copenhagen and Austria and then I'd let my family take care of the bills later." She laughs, clutching the cereal box to her chest.

If we had been born somewhere other than This Place and if we were people of a different regional temperament, I might've told her that, really, based on what I'd just experienced, if you were terminally ill and had only months to live, the last thing you'd want to do is ramble through some foreign country by yourself unable to avoid watching couples and families walk past on board-walks or sit in cafés—people healthy, tanned, and muscular—whose seeming wholeness and joviality and trinket-buying ways only serve to provide a depressing contrast to the lack of life you have left and underscore the reality of your impending death. The last thing you would want to do when ticking down the months, weeks, days, and hours of your life is to sit on a plane for seven-plus hours. The last thing you would want to do is discover everything you haven't seen and be faced with the reality that you never will.

Even if you do go, the steroids you take will strip you of muscle so quickly that within days coffee carafes will quiver in your hands. With weeks, you will move in slow motion, unable to pick yourself off the floor when you fall. In a month, the treatment you receive will bald you. Your body's simultaneous agency and deterioration will astound you.

But this is only the start—this is what happens in Spain. By the time you reach Copenhagen you sprout more tumors through-out your body like mysterious sand dunes cropping up overnight that you examine in a hotel mirror under the dim, flickering fluo-rescent light. You cannot fathom this person in the mirror before you. Boxed in by horror, you will not leave your hotel room. You will lust to be home and feel foolish for ever leaving because you now know—this isn't brain cancer. You've been misdiagnosed.

You will not lounge by the water or drink cappuccinos with a croissant or saunter through museums. Imaginary visions of this illness will be your obsession. By the time you get to Austria, you will be unable to crawl out of bed, stinking in your pajamas because you are now incontinent, your body pillaged by this enigmatic disease.

When you reach wherever you planned to go next, if you get there, you will be calling your family, shaken and afraid. *Please—come and get me.* Even then, depending on where those sand dunes cropped up, you might not even be able to do this.

Actually, your family has been calling you, asking how you are, asking what you've seen. *When are you coming home?*

But you cannot respond. You sit slumped forward in your hotel room bed, your mind corrupted, you speak of myths in languages you invented. You sleep for hours on end until you—

Your family will come to get your body and they will pay off your credit card vacation with what you've left behind in your estate. Their existence, too, will be made ironic by the tourists strolling through the city center bounding along with tote bags and sand-sprinkled towels. Your children will sort through the clothing you brought with you and wonder, *Why didn't she ever tell us she wanted to go to Vienna?* You will take no pictures, buy no souvenirs, get no sunburns. You will die in a foggy regret, your family baffled as to why you left then and why you left now.

Eileen's hands grow loose around the cereal box. She grins.

I grin back.

The ice cream bucket drips onto the floor. How could Eileen have known? She didn't know. I didn't tell her. And that wasn't her fault.

"You should go now, Eileen. I bet it's more fun."

As I walk through the front door back home, I see Donny sleeping belly up on the couch, his arms flailed static above him, as though caught in mid-dance. I tiptoe to shove the ice cream in the freezer and slither through the cracked door of my mother's room to set the diapers on her dresser.

Under the covers, my mother rattles, a maraca rolling across the floor.

I watch, heartache rising within me.

She rattles in and out. In and out.

I close my eyes and calculate the odds of ever speaking with her again.

Ten percent . . .
Six percent . . .
Three percent . . .
Zero? Zero.

Opening my eyes, I look at her again—my friend, my confidant, my guide to This Place.

My mother.

And I burst.

Say Hello to Your Grandparents Before They Fly Away!

Your Reading For: May 4, 2013

Dear Aries, this daily reading, while cast, will never have been seen by you. You will be awoken by the sound of your stepfather pounding on your door. You will watch him collapse into your brother's arms. You will know what has happened during the night. This is all the reading you need to do for today.

The lake pulsates taciturn before Donny and me. Still wearing our pajamas, we sit with our backs against the house, legs splayed in front of us on the deck as two cardinals flit around the yard. The birds zing from branch to branch, their red bodies brilliant against the monotone landscape.

The "insensitive" time is happening. They are taking her body away.

"There's Della and Albert," Donny whispers.

"There they are," I reply.

Later that night, I pretend to be in love.

After the show, I give Richard a ride home.

We climb into my car, slam the doors shut, and sit in silence, the keys heavy in my lap.

"How was your day?" I whisper.

He grabs my hand and squeezes.

"Better than yours."

Actors

Your Reading For: May 5, 2013
  Remember, stricken one, comfort can come in
many forms. Do not turn away from the arms that
embrace you.

Today is the last matinee.
    Once the show is over, three men with cordless drills disassemble the production's fake cabin in twelve minutes flat. Sawdust flies. Someone turns the radio on and Neil Diamond sings about Sweet Caroline against the squealing of power drills. We throw our sweat-stained blouses and six-weeks-unwashed pants into a rust-pocked washer in the theater's basement. The men pound stray nails out of the flats and assemble them into a pile to be stowed in a mysterious crevice of the theater until the next production, when they will be painted over and put up again. The bare walls of the theater reveal the accumulated moments of boredom waiting backstage: messages scrawled on the walls, collages created on cork boards, tattered paperback romance novels stacked in corners.

Someone hands me a power drill and tells me to start on the table stage left.

I pass the drill to Richard and decided to hide in the bathroom. That's where Dorothy finds me.

Dorothy is the group sales manager and director's wife who has vaguely known me since I was fourteen and friends with her daughter, Sharon, in high school. Dorothy manages to always look disheveled and glamorous at the same time—her hair isn't combed but she wears a cubic zirconia ring. There's lipstick on her front teeth, but her nails are lacquered. Her socks don't match, but her jacket is ironed and adorned with a bedazzled cameo brooch. She runs around the theater red-faced and grinning, always on some urgent, unknown mission with a clipboard in her hand and pen behind her ear.

Today, when Dorothy ran into the women's bathroom, she found me cross-legged underneath the baby-changing station staring at the linoleum floor with my left hand in my right. I was working through each finger absentmindedly massaging between the joints one by one, a pile of wadded toilet paper nestled in my lap.

We met eyes.

"My mom died yesterday."

She takes me to the dinner theater's back porch overlooking This Place's west side. The landscape's palette remains a hopeless spectrum of soggy brown dotted with the occasional green pine from a spring that has been trying to break since March only to be continually clobbered by snowstorms. Dorothy hands me a glass of water and sits next to me on a white plastic lawn chair while everyone else works back in the theater as her husband yells about the strike taking too long.

I watch the ice cubes shuffle around one another in my glass, my throat tightening to a toothpick.

I inhale.

"Dorothy, didn't you get married out here?"

I remember her telling me about it years ago.

"Oh, yes, we sure did. Right out here. Right over there in that gazebo."

She continues on, telling me about the ceremony, the gown, how her life has revolved around this dinner theater. I exhale.

"You know, sometimes I wonder if Sharon will get married out here. She's gotta boyfriend now. They're real serious."

Inhale.

"You wanna know something real interesting about him?" she asks.

"Yeah," I reply, turning to look at her.

She leans toward me and whispers.

"He's got *albinism.*"

"He's . . . albino?"

"*Yes.* He *is.*" She widens her eyes and reclines back in her chair. Icicles melt off rain gutters behind us. Runoff splatters on the sidewalk and clangs against the thick foliage of the overgrown yew shrubs that line the building. I start to ramble, "My parents had their reception here too. In October 1979 I think . . . And last Easter, my mom and stepfather and I came here for lunch and we sat out here."

I remember the glossy Polaroid picture of my mother and father on their wedding day. My mother with a white bonnet and plump face standing arm-in-arm with my father in a white leisure suit and bleached blonde hair. I remember the photo I took of my mother and Bruce in this very spot last spring—my mother grinning with a vodka tonic in one hand and her other arm around Bruce's waist, and Bruce, chain-smoking, in a deep purple sweater, his red hair mussed in the wind. I remember my mother sitting behind me while Elvis swaggered before us. I remember Bruce holding her as she walked out of the theater when she saw our show in March, her emaciated frame shuffling through the parking lot. I envision myself glazed-over in the women's bathroom minutes ago and I swear I'm going to choke and die right in this moment. My lungs swell with concrete. I'm going to asphyxiate and die. I can't breathe. The concrete hardens. Right here, right now, conc—

Dorothy grabs my elbow and I exhale.

"And now—I'm here," I squeak.

"And, now, you're here," Dorothy says with a gentleness and kindness so sincere that those four words and the glass of melted ice water in my hand and her just sitting here with me babbling about the two trivial anecdotes I know about this dinner theater where she's made her life make me want to crawl across the arms of our lawn chairs, throw myself across her like a baby rhesus monkey clinging to its mother, and sob into her perm. *Please— don't—leave—me.*

"Do you want to help me with something?" Dorothy asks.

"Okay."

She ushers me to the kitchen where she retrieves two bottles of champagne from an imposing stainless steel industrial fridge.

"We always have a toast after strike for everyone as a 'thank you' for their work on the show," she tells me as she grabs a cloth napkin to open the bottles with. She hands me a package of plastic champagne flutes to assemble. I rip the package open and start to stick the flimsy stems in the flute bases. She twists the bottle and whispers.

"I didn't know your mom was sick."

". . . I didn't know—how to say it."

The cork pops.

Dorothy grabs the second bottle and I coach myself to be able to hand the flutes out, *Hurray! It's the end!*

"I wish I would've known. I had no idea this was going on with you . . ."

A burst of laughter reverberates from the theater as I think, *I'm a good actor.*

Birthday

Your Reading For: May 6, 2013
    Little Ram, yes, this may feel devastating. But
this is not the end.

The strike at home begins and I am in charge of costumes. Bruce and Donny are in charge of the party.

Once they leave to pick out flowers and get their suits dry-cleaned, I inch into my mother's bedroom, her voice echoing within me—*Soon all of this will be yours* . . . Her perfume hangs in the air, stray hairs gleam on the pillows. Her belongings remain scattered throughout the room and I am crazed with simultaneous questions and answers. Is she somewhere here? *Of course not.* Is that why it smells like her? *Nope, you saw her leave.* Was it all an illusion, a stunt? *No, you watched the coroner drive away.* If I were to go into her closet, would I find her there smirking at me? The grand prank revealed?

I tense up to bolt to her closet and—*No. She died. She's gone.*

More possibilities surface—*Maybe she left me something. Maybe there's a message written to me in her coat pockets, a letter left at the back of the closet, a symbol waiting for me. Maybe there's something . . .*

I run to her closet and fling the door open. I am rabid. Wild. I have grown claws, sprouted fur. I foam at the mouth. I plunge my hands into her coat pockets, searching. I find melted peppermints, a five-dollar bill, and crumpled receipts. I shake out all of her shoes. Dirt and pine needles fall to the floor. I dig through her purses and turn them over and there's nothing but lipstick tubes. I look through her nursing scrubs to see if something is stuck between them. I smear my face in her scratchy winter sweaters and run their rough fibers against my neck like a loofa. I wrap the legs of pressed jeans and worn corduroys and pajamas matted with her own hair around my torso. I throw all of the clothes onto the floor, run my hands along the shelves, and rip clothes off their hangers.

I dig. I shake the fabrics. I look inside sleeves. I look inside pant legs. I rifle through skirt tulle. I search for something—anything. And there's nothing. Nothing but a daughter desperately searching.

Under the sink . . .

I run to it, sit on my knees, and open the cabinet doors.

It's nearly barren.

I piece through the items. There's a pair of black tights, the last dose in a three-day yeast infection treatment kit, and a birthday card for my twenty-fifth birthday that she never gave me.

Happy Birthday to My Daughter on Her 25th Year . . .

This could be my message.

My sign.

My antidote.

Fingers trembling, nearly electric, I open the card . . .

It's blank.

There's nothing written inside.

I open the card wider, its edges sliding against my palms. The shadow of a crease disappears into further emptiness.

She left me a blank card.

My breath dissolves. I curl forward unable to move until, somehow, breath fills me and all I can manage to do is wail—and I wail and wail until shallow inhalations move staccato through me. Curling into a ball, I let the card slip from my fingers and imagine my body as a desert floor, cracked and thirsty for a rain that will never fall.

~~Vicky~~

Your Reading For: May 7, 2013
   Your mother always told you that you should've
gone into writing. Though she probably didn't think
you'd do it in this way.

The microwave clock glows 4:57 am. Bruce's laptop sits dim before me. Wrapped in a blanket and stocking feet, I place my hands on the keyboard and continue to type, stale crumbs snapping beneath the pressure of my typing fingers.
Save as "Working Draft—Mom Obituary"

Victoria L. "Vicky" Ness, age 57, of Chippewa Falls, ~~died, transitioned into the spirit world,~~ passed away ~~in her bed~~ at home on May 4, 2013, following a ~~heartbreaking, painful,~~ brief ~~stint experience with~~ battle with ~~misdiagnosed lymphoma that originated in her brain~~ cancer. She was surrounded by ~~her nightstand and snoring husband, Arch Angel Michael, no one,~~ her ~~shocked, often bombed, sleeping, confused and oblivious~~ loving family. ~~She was beautiful, fun, and carefree.~~
   ~~Vicky was a devout Catholic. Vicky was interested in occult spiritualities.~~ Vicky was born February 26, 1956, in Chippewa Falls, the ~~accidental child~~ youngest daughter of Albert and Della (Ryan) LaFaive ~~who cooked her pet rabbit in a stew and made her get a perm every Easter. Interestingly, she thought her parents reincarnated into the two cardinals that visited her backyard overlooking grand Lake Wissota.~~ She attended Holy Ghost elementary school. ~~During her childhood years, her~~

~~wrists were slapped by nuns and she watched her class-~~
~~mates puke in the cathedral's balcony because it was so~~
~~hot. When not at church, she played with her beloved~~
~~pet Chihuahua named Sputnik.~~ She graduated from
McDonell High School in 1974. ~~There she met a young~~
~~man who didn't know how to pull out or use a condom~~
~~leaving her to learn the ins and outs of the adoption sys-~~
~~tem and driving alone to abortion clinics in Minneapolis~~
~~by the time she turned twenty. These pregnancies would~~
~~leave her with a tiny candle of guilt lit inside her that~~
~~only those who were closest could see.~~ She attended
Chippewa Valley Technical College ~~and during this time~~
~~she met a man who had paid attention during Sex Ed.~~
~~and would eventually father the children she would raise~~
~~nine years later~~, becoming a Licensed Practical Nurse and
furthered her education to become a Registered Nurse
~~where she ate various donuts studying for her exams that~~
~~she would later sweat off through furious aerobics classes~~
~~wearing spandex in her mid-twenties.~~ Her places of work
include: the Northern Center, Dove Health Care, Sacred
Heart Hospital, and, most recently, ~~she looked at people's~~
~~colons in~~ Mayo Clinic in the Pre and Post Operative
Recovery Unit. There she developed special bonds with
her coworkers, both professionally and socially.

Vicky married Tom Kersten in 1979 and had two
children from this marriage. They later divorced ~~less~~
~~than a year after their son was born after they accused~~
~~one another of cheating on each other. Vicky hired the~~
~~best damn lawyer in Western Wisconsin and took half of~~
~~everything plus joint custody.~~ In 1993, she married Bruce
Ness ~~who tenderly took care of her in the final months of~~
~~her life.~~

~~Vicky liked to relax on her daughter's bed, read~~
~~about her ex-husband's natal chart, and giggle about his~~
~~eccentricities. Vicky liked to play slot machines and~~
~~drink into the wee hours of the morning and crawl into~~
~~bed stinking like cigarettes and perfume, her mind awash~~
~~with memories of slow-dances and neon lights. Vicky~~
~~was a gentle woman who liked flowers and animals. She~~

~~liked to purchase pets on a whim. Her most spontaneous~~
~~purchase was a pair of hedgehogs who eventually escaped~~
~~from the makeshift chicken-wire corral in her family's~~
~~backyard. Their skeletons were later found underneath~~
~~the neighbor's deck.~~ She was ~~a partier, a sun worshipper,~~
an avid reader who also enjoyed ~~boozing, gambling,~~
gardening and walking her dogs ~~who she liked to feed~~
~~cheeseburgers from the McDonald's drive-thru.~~ She
loved to spend ~~money on new swimming suits, trips to~~
~~the Caribbean with her husband, and cashmere sweaters,~~
summer days with her friends and family on Lake Wissota: ~~sunburnt, buzzed, and chatting,~~ dining out, playing
games, and boating. ~~She spent her winters soaking in hot~~
~~baths and lighting candles, dreaming of hot white sand~~
~~beneath her feet and retirement at the age of 62.~~

She is survived by her husband Bruce ~~who loved her~~
~~so dearly,~~ son Donny Kersten ~~who's going to marry the~~
~~Oklahoma version of her,~~ daughter Courtney Kersten
~~who,~~ three sisters and many ~~other people who you only~~
~~see at family reunions~~ nieces and nephews.

~~And most ironically considering she was the youngest~~
~~daughter, the only people~~ She was preceded in death by
~~are~~ her parents~~, the cardinals.~~

I sit back.

The cursor blinks.

I pull my arms in front of me, grab my elbows, and rest my
forehead on my arms. My unwashed hair reaches forward onto
my forearm like a thick paperback falling open. Cocking my head
to the right, I stare out across the naked backyard as the sun breaks
over the horizon.

Where are the cardinals?

Vacant branches undulate against the breeze.

All this blankness.

A homesickness—for her, for guidance, for credulous belief—
swells inside me and I close my eyes. I imagine my mother's
whirling handwriting across the lake, up the bank, through her
obituary, and onto a blank card. I imagine her words rushing
through me. I imagine being saturated in understanding.

Kneel

Your Reading For: May 10, 2013
    Little Ram, take solace in this: sometimes you must journey to find the irony. Allow for levity to arise on this day. Your mother wouldn't have wanted it any other way.

My mother's funeral takes place at a Catholic cathedral in the middle of a cornfield. The sanctuary has high vaulted ceilings and ornate gold-painted detail throughout the church. Years before, my mother bought me a royal purple silk blouse that I'd never worn. I felt there'd never been an occasion special enough to wear a silk shirt.

This is special enough.

Donny, Bruce, my father, and I sit in the front row and the service begins. Organ chords boom and I shift in my seat, sit bones hard against the wooden pew. Next to me, my father gulps. I hand him a tissue. I imagine a synthesizer, Steve Perry crooning "Who's Crying Now," and the drone of radio static. My father blows his nose, punctuates it with a trumpet-like note, and holds the tissue between his hands as though he were cupping an injured sparrow until he is overtaken again and dabs the paper blob under his eyes. He eventually takes off his glasses and I know, given that we have the exact same prescription, everything is fuzzy beyond comprehension.

I focus on everything I don't understand—the elaborate robes, the ritual, the incense, my relatives drinking wine straight from the chalice. I don't know when to kneel or not kneel, when to bow my head or not bow my head. I don't understand what the incense has to do with anything, but I like watching the smoke billow, grow, and disappear. The third time the congregation, including my father and Donny, somehow they know, churn forward to kneel with an audible clamor, I whisper to Bruce behind my program.

"How do we know when we're supposed to kneel? Are we supposed to kneel?"

"We're not kneeling," he hisses.

And we sit tall and motionless like telephone poles while the entire congregation rolls back and forth behind us like oarsmen rowing toward the end of the service.

Afterwards, it's decaf and chicken dinner at a local diner. It's shots and cigarettes in the alley. It's relatives swarming and flowers ferried from this table to that table. It's snotty tissues and empty beer bottles sitting beside the centerpieces. It's me staring into a mound of mashed potatoes and gravy. It's sticking a spoon into the center like a flag and declaring it my temporary truce.

Later that night as I hang my silk shirt, I see two strands of light wafting in the fabric as I lace the shoulders onto the hanger's edges. From hugging and greeting people, the two back seams have split and hang shredded.

I start to smile.

And then I nearly fall to my knees.

Holes.

Pit

Your Reading For: June 5, 2013
If you think that relying on the advice of your aloof Norwegian ancestors is a sound way to mourn in the Midwest, you must understand that your aloof Norwegian ancestors also ate raw herring, acidified pudding, and fish soaked in lye. Use this information to determine the validity of their advice accordingly, young Aries.

I begin to fill the blankness by co-teaching elementary school students Reader's Theater for the summer. We meet in the mornings and afternoons at a local elementary school and have lunch on the playground with snacks at 10:30 a.m. and 2 p.m. We teach the students how to impersonate zoo animals, make newspaper capes, and highlight their lines. We never rehearse. Scripts are lost and recovered on a daily basis. The little girls bicker with each other over who gets to play the jester or the willow tree and the boys make cardboard swords and whack one another with them. The children critique each other during the five minutes we try to rehearse before we perform for the classroom next door and they flit around with strips of paper stuck to them with stiff masking tape. The classroom floor is a continual mess of paper scraps and wads of tape and forgotten pen tops. And one child imitating a cow mooing spreads through the room like a weird infectious disease until all seventeen of them are mooing.

I am a place-marker of a teacher. I wander and watch the kids without comment. Sometimes a little boy or girl will ask me to cut something for them—a circle or something thin and curvy or a letter—or ask me to help them find their script which is invariably either on the playground, in a bathroom stall, or trapped under a desk. Sometimes they ask me to watch them spin in a circle as their construction-paper costumes float in the air around them. I do not pick up the scripts I see smashed underneath chair legs or find the caps for the markers or break up their bickering over who should play the willow tree. When they moo or cluck or bark as a unit, I listen and smile and let someone else protest that this is getting too loud or too stupid. And when they are silent again and return to cutting, or when they run around the room, screaming about missing their bumblebee stinger, I feel secure. The chaos is comforting.

Grief has been stalking me for weeks, I imagine her peeping through the shades, hiding in the woods, following me around town in a rust-eaten, champagne Chevy Lumina minivan, studying my habits, smoking menthols, and scribbling notes in her palm, waiting for the exact wrong moment to make her appearance. Today, I am crouched on the carpeting, showing a little boy how to use a tape dispenser.

"Press down with your thumb and pull the tape off with your other hand," I tell him as I look up to see her through the window, climbing over a hedge. She waves and points to indicate that she's going through the front doors. I shake my head.

No. No, you're not.

She goes around the hedge and within seconds, I am clobbered by the scent of my mother's perfume, her fine china fingers placing loose hair behind my ear, her voice down the hallway. Face in hands, I leak through my fingers while the little boy watches, the tape dispenser sprawled loose on the floor. I repeat my mantra. *My palms are sponges. My palms are sponges. My palms are sponges.*

Found me.

Grief extinguishes her cigarette in the potted plant, steps over the yellow kiddie chairs, and throws herself against me. She twists, squeezes, and wrings me out, a listless dishrag beaten against the side of a steel sink. She breathes in my ear, *It's best if this doesn't happen in front of the children.*

I tell the little boy I'm sorry, but I have to go right now and I scuttle out of the room.

We go to the bathroom and I slide against the wall to sit on the floor. Head to knees, exhaling and inhaling into denim, I can fall apart here.

Okay. Choke me. Strangle me. Just do it.

"Miss Courtney, are you okay?"

I look up.

She followed me, the one who's always looking for her script.

This is one of my new best friends. She is nine years old and as uncomplicated as a snow cone. The first day of class she told me she liked my earrings and I told her I liked her sneakers so that means we're friends.

"Go. Please. You—can go. Unless—you have to pee or—something. I'm—okay."

She comes over to me.

"Why are you crying?"

I stare at her.

What do I tell you? Do I tell you about watching someone you love die slowly, painfully, torturously? Do I tell you about your reality eroding from the inside, a fungus that you can smell and see but cannot throw chemicals at to control? Do I tell you that each day is a continual Pit and to send down a canary and a jug of water?

"I won't tell. I promise."

I pause.

"I miss—I miss my mom."

She stares, her mouth agape, and twists her left foot against the tiled floor.

When you're a snow cone, there's nothing to say to that.

"You can go back to class. I'll be o—"

"No. I want to come with you. I'll walk next to you."

I smear my face in my shirt and stand up as she throws herself against me in a fierce hug. She has construction-paper claws taped around her hands and a red headpiece. She plays a lobster in our production. I am wearing a tail. They thought I needed a tail.

It looks like a psychedelic turd.

She grabs my hand and we walk back to class in silence.

It is our greatest performance.

Gimme

Your Reading For: July 12, 2013
   When looking up "machine shop" in the phone
book, the listing may be under "metalwork."

Bruce has replaced me.
   I return home after working the three-to-eleven evening shift at the hotel to find Donny and Bruce gathered around the kitchen table with a cornucopia of bottles, potato-chip bags, and scratch-offs lying between them. The cheese curds and rhubarb pies and gumbos have been gone since May. The total contents of our kitchen consists of Kool-Aid powder packets, baby carrots, and salted peanuts. My mother's warm home has morphed into a bachelor pad complete with dirty undershirts on the floor, empty beer cans on the counter, and piles of dirty dishes in the sink. The papier-mâché elephant is no longer a hip design choice but now a relic from a jungle-themed party three weeks ago.

As I walk in the front door, Donny and Bruce turn to look at me and shout my name in unison. Donny runs over to me with a beer in hand and ushers me to the kitchen table.

"We're going to do it!" Donny says, pulling out a chair for me.

"We're gonna do it," Bruce replies softer.

"Do what?" I ask.

"Spread the ashes! Spread the *ashes*!" Donny chants.

They are drunk. Bruce has crawled into The Pit with Donny. Welcome to the party.

Donny continues in a fervent monologue and had I not just walked in and observed the prior scene I would've thought he'd rehearsed it.

He begins.

"*Tomorrow*, we're gonna do it tomorrow. We're gonna take the urn to the lake and set it free. Because it doesn't matter. That's not *her*! That's just a buncha *stuff*. Just a buncha dust! She's not that *jar*. That's not *her* in the *jar*. We're not gonna worship some fucking jar. We gotta let her be free! Like a bird! Like a leaf! Like . . . I don't know. But, we gotta! Because Mom—was more than jar! She was a *lady*—a *good* lady. And . . . hey!"

He glares at Bruce and me.

"We gotta keep it together! None of this crying shit. None of it. She'd want us to be *happy*. Happy that we are still fuckin' *alive*. So no crying tomorrow! She wouldn't want it."

Donny sits back and takes a swig of his beer.

"Yeah, not her. Wouldn't want it," Bruce mumbles.

Regret plows through me for ever telling Donny about the time our mother and I slow danced to The Doors and she told me about wanting to be put in the lake. But as I sit at the table, before their tears and boozy exuberance, I feel powerless to protest.

I nod my head in agreement.

Let's spread the ashes tomorrow.

Two o'clock. Meet on the dock.

And when tomorrow is today, I wake at six a.m. to Donny sick in the bathroom from the previous evening's festivities. When I get up to check on him an hour later, he's passed out next to the shower. I put a towel over him and make the sign of the cross.

By eight, I'm sitting on the porch with Bruce while he smokes cigarette after cigarette.

By ten Donny has joined us and cracked the first of many beers. The breeze shuffles an already empty cigarette pack around the patio table.

By noon, both of them are in a state similar to last night.

I've moved to the kitchen to read the newspaper.

Two hours later, I ask them through the screen door if they really want to do this today and they roar back, "Yes—yes, we do! We're gonna get on the boat and do this! Jus' like she'd want!"

If I had the energy, maybe I would've suggested that we wait. I would've hid the urn in my closet. I would've reasoned that we should do this when we're feeling more stable, more sensitive, more sober.

Instead, I grab the urn and meet them in the backyard.

We traipse down the steps to the lake and climb onboard the battered pontoon. Donny gets behind the wheel and buzzes us into the middle of the lake, waves churning us up and down like a seesaw. Speedboats buzz, dragging screaming teenagers on inner tubes. Trout and bass glide beneath us. Two girls in a paddleboat struggle to make their way back to shore in the distance, zigzagging the entire way.

Donny kills the motor.

We pass the urn around and whisper sentences that no one else can hear but I'm assuming have to do with love and loss and promising to stop drinking so much. And Donny cries and Bruce cries and I cry. And Bruce smokes more cigarettes and we smear our faces on the back of our hands and even I crack a beer in honor of the moment. And once we've all recovered, I look at Bruce and he looks at the urn and back at me.

I get to open it.

I switch places with Donny so I'm in the driver's seat and put the urn between my legs, the flower engraving rough against my fingers.

"I'm gonna open it," I announce.

I place my hands around the smooth lid and turn it.

It doesn't budge.

I grip harder.

I gasp. I clench and turn and my hands slip.

It doesn't move.

I wipe my hands on my jeans and try again and my hands slide. It won't move.

I can't open it.

Donny stands up in a huff.

"Gimme it, Court."

I pass it to him.

He grabs the urn and holds it between his legs.

He tries to turn the lid just as I had but it doesn't move—his fingers slide around the rim.

He groans and wipes his hands on his jeans and tries one more time.

His muscles bulge. His elbows shake.

He can't open it.

Bruce stands up.

"Gimme it, Donny."

Donny hands it to Bruce.

He sticks the urn in the crook of his arm and tries to turn the lid.

It doesn't twist.

He tries again and his fingers skid.

"*Jesus* Christ—"

"Gimme it, Bruce," I say and we all try one more time. From me to Donny to Bruce—each of us grunting and glistening, hands red and puffy—and we can't open it.

Then Donny and Bruce try together—Bruce holds the bottom and twists and Donny holds the top and twists.

The urn will not open.

Bruce wipes perspiration off his brow.

Donny keeps looking at that urn as though his gaze alone could twist the top off.

I look across the horizon, to the speedboats and the fisherman and those girls in the paddleboat. Do these people see us stumbling around this boat trying to open this brass monster of an urn? Do they wonder what we're doing floating around the middle of this lake? Do they know that we're dumping our dead mother into the lake and that she was insistent that we do this? Do they realize this is supposed to be a sacred *moment* that's being hijacked by our inability to open this cast iron battle-axe?

I take a sip of my beer. It's disgusting.

I pipe up, "What if we banged the top of the urn against the bottom of the boat—that's what I do when I can't open a jar of peanut butter. It might help dislodge the—"

"That is *sacrilegious*, Courtney Ann. That's your mother in there."

We all glare at the urn.

"They must've soldered it shut," Donny mutters. "Wh—*why* did they solder it shut?" Donny throws himself into the driver's seat, "That fucking funeral home. Sealing it shut . . . Fuck!"

Water laps against the pontoon.

"This isn't happening today," Donny concludes.

"Nope," Bruce mutters. "Not today."

I stagger over to the urn, wrap it in a Mickey Mouse towel, and hold it in my lap. Donny starts the pontoon engine and we turn back toward the dock, the urn a silent, hermetic baby in my arms.

We cruise back toward shore and I wonder why the urn won't open. Isn't this a typical ritual? Spreading ashes? Why would they melt it shut? Was it—a *sign*? That my mother wasn't meant to be put in this lake? Did she want to be put somewhere else? A different Deep End? Or did it mean that she didn't want to be put in any Deep End at all? That the whole experience we had years ago was just a joke? A momentary fantasy?

We pull into the dock.

I hug the urn closer to my chest, the phrase *I don't know* scrolling through me.

Four Hours

Your Reading For: August 4, 2013

Baby Ram, this may be hard to imagine for you are a creature of a different sort, but remember chameleons are not the patterns they appropriate but the skin beneath their changing pigmentation. What are you at the core?

Judge Judy is talking through the floorboards. I hear her above me, scolding a plaintiff about her questions only requiring a yes or a no while Bruce drunkenly makes spaghetti. Sprawled on my bedroom floor, I envision the scene: him shuffling around, the sauce bubbling and splattering, the noodles missing the colander and sliding into the sink, Judge Judy breaking for commercials—*An Everything Must Go Mattress Sale! Low APR Financing*... And then I see it: the newspaper still folded on the kitchen countertop next to the ever-increasing mound of unopened mail. *The newspaper*... Lying flat on my back against the floor, my eyes ping open.

I crawl to my feet, flip the light off, and patter up the stairs to peer out at Bruce in the kitchen.

He sings to himself, slicing an economy-sized block of cheddar cheese with a mandolin. The television blares. There's a sale on chicken at the local grocery store. A public service announcement about leaving dogs in hot cars. The newspaper is where I envisioned it to be: unopened and waiting on the countertop. I slink over to it, avoiding Bruce's gaze, grab the paper, and stick it in my back pocket as I go back downstairs.

I open the door to my bedroom and grope for the light switch. Finding it, I illuminate my dilemma: an open suitcase and the entirety of my mother's clothing and my possessions strewn throughout the room. It's midnight and I'm leaving for northern Idaho in four hours to start graduate school and I am frenzied and paranoid—I've been agonizing all day about what to bring and not to bring, the hypotheticals of life in Idaho blossoming into nightmares contingent upon what I decide to put in this suitcase.

Do I need this amethyst turtle figurine?

Do I need these books about planetary cycles? What if I need to know the whereabouts of Jupiter or Saturn?

Should I bring my mother's nursing scrubs? Why would I need nursing scrubs?

What about my mother's saint statues from the Catholic church? What if I need to look at Saint Bernadette?

What about my mother's jeans? They don't fit. I can't wear them, but what if I could one day? What if I might want to have them? What if one night I was awake and longed to bury my face in them, to be close to her belongings?

What if—

And so on for hours. I've considered each item bequeathed to me and each token I've clutched. Despite any prior oscillation or doubt, the thought of moving without them leaves me nauseated. Can I truly forge onward without something to cling to, whether it be my mother's belongings or my accumulated theories about the universe? Can I continue spinning without these objects in my orbit?

Then there's that pile of newspaper horoscope clippings I've collected since January currently sitting under a rock on my nightstand.

I step over a pile of my mother's shoes—items that, again, don't fit, but I can't bear to part with—to sit cross-legged on my bed and open the classifieds. I skim—lawnmowers for sale, dental technicians needed in Rice Lake, telemarketing jobs available in Strum, free kittens downtown, and so on until I reach the last page.

It's now 12:24 a.m.

Yesterday's column reads:

> Dear Aries!
> You may bump into an old friend today who
> will bring up old wounds. Forgiveness is your
> namesake today.

An old friend?

Is this a reference to Judge Judy? That rerun blaring through the floorboards? Or is this in reference to the bottle of gin Bruce found in the back of the pantry? Or is this "old friend" all of my mother's belongings? The lacy bras? The shoulder pads? Is this in reference to Bruce? My old friend: drunken Bruce? Or is this just another nebulous reading to add to my ever-increasing pile of horoscope clippings?

I glare at the newspaper clippings on my nightstand, fan my arms across the bed to grab them and pull them toward me. Enter the astrology assemblage. I scroll through them like an animation flip book.

> Dear Aries!
> Familial matters may get heated today. Remember to take time and space for—

> Dear Aries!
> Have you been feeling lonely? Now is the time for romance! Why no—

> Dear Aries!
> Spirits are high on this day; any financial worries should be put aside for—

> Dear Aries!
> Do not let your impulsivity get ahead of you during the holi—

> Dear Aries!
> You are prone to head injuries. Be especially cautious—

Has any of this actually helped me? There's no story or secret message here—why have I been collecting these? Shouldn't I be my own authority on what I need? And if I clearly can't put my faith into this, then why am I agonizing over jeans and shoulder pads? I stare at my hands, my fingertips smudged with ink.

What am I doing?

I stuff the newspaper clippings under the bed, hop up, and start to throw items into the suitcase from around the room. A bra. A pair of my mother's underwear. Some socks. A bathing suit. Tweezers. A book on how to train Labrador retrievers. Wool socks—

I pause, holding the socks in my hand.

If there was a newspaper horoscope clipping that could help me right now, what would it say?

It would probably tell me to go to bed. *Dear Aries! Sleep is nigh!*

I toss the socks into the suitcase and trudge upstairs where Judy Judy screams about child support. Bruce sits before her, twirling noodles on a fork. I call to him from across the kitchen.

"Hi, Bruce."

"Hi, Court!"

He turns around, waves, and pivots back to Judge Judy. I pivot to the laundry room to find a piece of paper and pen. Bruce's briefcase vibrates on top of the dryer. I open it, find a legal pad, grab a pen, and write a goodbye note for him to read in the morning. Using the washer as a desk, I thank him for letting me stay here, for keeping all of us afloat the past eight months, and for being my stepfather. I tell him I'll see him in December and as I finish the note, I prop my chin in my palm for a moment to rest and nearly pass out in the mere seconds perched there.

I go to Bruce and tap his shoulder.

"Bruce, I'm going to bed now—my dad's picking me up in a few hours and driving me to the airport."

Bruce gasps and wipes sauce off his face.

"You're leaving?"

"Yes."

"Well! Guh! How are you going to get to the airport?"

". . . Tom's driving me."

Bruce stands up and hugs me, sauce and cheese glistening on his bathrobe, and he tells me he hopes I have a good trip. I tell him he'll see me one more time—I'm going to haul my suitcase up here before I go to bed.

I tromp back downstairs and keep throwing items at random into the suitcase until it's full, too fatigued to care about what's in it. I shove the rest of my mother's clothing and my belongings into the closet, toss a bunch of books on top of the mess, and lug the suitcase up the stairs. When I make my way to the top, I scan the room and see Bruce is gone. I check the bathroom, the garage, his bedroom. The door is closed.

Snores rumble behind the door.

An infomercial for the Magic Bullet blares on the television behind me, chopping garlic, onions, and beans. I leave my note to Bruce underneath the coffeepot, shut the television off, put the spaghetti sauce and noodles in the fridge, clean up the spills and stray mushrooms, shut the lights off, and feel my way back down the stairs to my bedroom where I crawl into bed and collapse into unconsciousness.

Hours later, I leave. From This Place to Minneapolis, from a layover in Phoenix to a layover in Seattle to the Washington/Idaho border, where I find myself sitting on my suitcase before a sprawling wheat field, waiting for a taxi, when Bruce calls me.

"Hi, Bruce."

"Courtney! I just got your note. When did you leave?"

"Last night. Or—this morning."

"You did?"

"Yeah. Tom picked me up and took me to the airport. I said goodnight to you."

". . . You did?"

"Yeah. You were watching *Judge Judy* and making spaghetti."

"I was?"

"Yeah."

"Well . . . Guess that explains where the spaghetti came from."

"Yeah."

". . . Well."

The phone line crackles.

A crow squawks in the distance.

"I guess I don't remember any of that."

"Oh, well . . . That's okay, Bruce."

I watch the wind roll a tumbleweed through the ditch.

"There's a lot I don't want to remember, Court . . ."

". . . Sure. I—I understand, Bruce."

We hang up.

I stare into the wheat field, each slope tumbling into the next slope, as apprehension rises within me and I feel as though I might be drowning in this wheat field, choking on the stalks, submerged and gasping for air. I don't—I don't know what to do, how to live, who I should be. I want a reading. I want a guide. I want a buoy to cling to. I want a sign, something to fall from the sky, or come crawling from the ditch—an animal or a stray dog or a bird to signal that the world is in balance, life is proceeding as planned, that I am fine.

Was the tumbleweed a sign?

I look for it.

It's running away from me, sprinting down the ditch.

I have no reading, no mother, no symbolic tumbleweed. What did I bring with me? What do I have? I don't even know where I am. Didn't I call a taxi?

And at that moment, if I could've had a reading, if the sky could've opened up and spoken to me through a cosmic intercom, if I could've read the texture of wheat and translated it, this is what it would have said:

> Sweet impetuous Aries!
>
> What an autumn in store for you! Have you noticed things falling apart? From your clothing to your relationships, do things seem to be slowly unraveling more and more each day? Don't fret, dear Aries, you're just in the midst of your Own Personal Retrograde! And remember—in case you've forgotten your astrology studies, despite any unease this may cause, a retrograde is merely an illusion! You've probably been feeling the effects for

several months now, a distinct stillness where those feelings of intuition, belief, and knowingness may have slipped away into the oblivion . . .

The feeling continues to crest, growing higher and higher, I'm flooded in this alien landscape and I'm frantic. I dig my hand into the suitcase, groping for something—a rock or a figurine or anything. I start pulling—underwear, a shampoo bottle, those wool socks . . .

Are you sure you want to dump out all of your things on the airport sidewalk? This isn't going to help—you left all your woo-woo worldly goods back home. Anyway, sweet Aries, get ready for the debris to fall! You are gliding into the peak of this phenomenon—remember to wear a headlamp! It may be even harder to see your path during the following period. So, in true retrograde spirit, rather than making any grand assumptions about the nature of the universe, sit tight during this time, hold your conclusions in suspension and do not make any of those impulsive decisions that you are so prone to making. This is a time when your false assumptions and fears will come to the surface for you to examine.

I zip the suitcase open and peer inside. My mother's socks; a plastic water bottle; an orange extension cord. Why did I bring an extension cord? I flip the suitcase open.

Meanwhile, in Idaho you will look across sloping wheat fields, topography you've never seen before, and feel like you are stranded on Mars. You will meet other young people who have lost their parents in what seems like droves—this woman who lost her mother at age eleven, this man who lost his mother at sixteen, this guy who lost his father at twenty-three, this lady who lost her father at eighteen—and when they ask you how you are, you'll tell them that you feel like you're living on Mars. And they'll reply, yes, you probably do feel that way.

I start peeling back the layers. I peel away my mother's bedazzled jackets and the faux-fur vest. I peel away the book about training Labrador retrievers. I peel away her bras that I threw into the suitcase for some inexplicable reason . . .

> In Idaho, your mother's clothing will become the altar to which you pray. You will wear her clothing religiously and with it, you will outstretch your arms into your very own sea anemone pose, hoping to graze that person you long to see, hoping to persuade the cosmos to let you in on the secrets your mother never spoke to you—her ability to laugh at paper-ring-making psychics, her carefree ability to sunbathe in the driveway at two in the afternoon. You will ask her blouses, sweaters, and bra straps to give you her wisdom, to tell you what she would've told you as though they could open their little fabric mouths and whisper all the answers . . .

Where are the rocks? Where are my books? Where is my collection of pennies that I thought could be tokens from the universe?

> Do not be so naïve as to think your mother's sweater will tell you anything, dear Aries. It's time to stop relying on your possessions—her possessions—for answers.
>   In Idaho, you will be paranoid about tumors and breast tissue and whatever stuff might be lurking in your shampoo. You will be paranoid of dying at twenty-seven or thirty-seven or forty-seven or

fifty-seven. You'll be terrified of your body. You'll make an appointment to see a doctor.

During which, a nurse will call your name and hold the door open for you. You will walk toward her and within seconds of seeing this nurse in baby blue scrubs, the memory of your mother's scrubs will waft over you—her folding them, her perched at the kitchen table drinking a beer after work still in them, and you picking them up in her closet, now yours. And walking there with that nurse, you will start to panic. To choke up. To tremble.

The nurse will take you back to the examination room and the hallway will be flooded with them: women wandering in scrubs. Like bees. Like wasps. Locusts swarming.

I flip the entire suitcase over onto the sidewalk and start to search, flinging objects, trying to see if my mother's saint figurines are hidden in a sock or sweater. I shake the water bottle—maybe something shimmied inside it. I smell her pajamas, hoping the scent will act like an elixir and calm me . . .

You won't be able to breathe.

The nurse will instruct you to sit in a plastic chair in the examining room and so you do. She'll look at your chart.

"So, Courtney. It looks like you're here for a—"

She'll gawk at you.

"What's wrong?"

Snot will ooze down your upper lip. Tears will drip off your chin. You'll swear you're going to quiver right off this chair. You will feel grotesque and ridiculous. You'll swear you're a mutant. You'll ask yourself, "Am I bawling, drowning in my own inability to breathe because there are people everywhere wearing baby blue nursing scrubs? Am I crying because of scrubs?"

Well, yes, dear Aries. Yes, you are.

And so you reply to the nurse.

"I'm upset—because there are—scrubs everywhere."

"You're upset because of scrubs?"

You fear she's going to send you in for a psychiatric evaluation. "Red flag!" The chart would read, "Twenty-five-year-old woman presented with manic fear of nursing scrubs. Request for 'checkup' was truly a cry for help—"

"No—No. My mom just—died. And she was a—nurse. And seeing scrubs—makes me sad. But, I'm—really—okay. So, you know, carry on! I'm—gonna be—fine," you'll say.

"Okay, well, just try to relax. . . . This isn't a crisis," she'll say, handing you a box of tissues.

I stand up, grab the suitcase and shake it, hoping something magical and spiritually sanctified falls out. And there's nothing. There's nothing here. I don't have anything from the Deep End with me. I've taken none of my occult tokens, it's all sitting shoved in my closet at home.

The nurse will ask you about your health history and if you're on any medication and if you're allergic to penicillin. You'll tell her your mother died of lymphoma and that your aunt and your cousin and great-grandmother had breast cancer. And, you guess, your mother did too. You'll tell her that you're not on any medication and you're not allergic to anything. Just pollen in August.

"The doctor will be in soon."

As soon as the door closes, the memories will smother you again. You'll collapse on the chairs and coach yourself to breathe. Ten minutes later someone knocks.

"It's Dr. Somethingoranother . . .?"

You'll sit up and cross your legs.

"Come in," you'll croak.

> The doctor will walk in, looking at your chart, and sit down.

I fall to my knees and howl.

> The doctor will look up and stare.
> You'll stare back and sniffle.
> She'll study you.
> "You're very emotional."
> She'll sit back in her chair and look at your chart again.
> "You didn't request a pregnancy test—did you need one?"
> And you will feel even more foolish—your sorrow taken as something hormonal, your emotions taken as a red flag, your concerns merely melodrama.

What—what am I doing?

> In Idaho, the effects of your retrograde will come into full force as the familiarity of This Place will somehow appear attractive, you'll long for those cheery conversations, those predictable pleasantries. You'll desire the ignorance of years past, to live in delusion, to be like Linda Goodman setting the table for her long disappeared and deceased kin.

I'm nothing but a deranged sandpiper looking for clams, chasing waves, running back and forth to the Deep End. When I think I've abandoned it for good, I only run back looking for sustenance and when I am there, I asphyxiate in doubt.

> As you turn your headlamp on and spelunk into the mystery of this retrograde, do not forget that, one day, when you least expect it, the path will become clear again and the answers to the questions

you carry within you will illuminate. But in this
period, be content with not only having to wear a
headlamp but with your light occasionally going
dark altogether.

A taxi drives up.

It's coming toward me.

I stand up, belongings dumped at my feet, my face ruddy and wet.

The driver rolls the window down, "You need some help?"

Me? Help? This woman bawling on the sidewalk, her suitcase overturned and meager belongings sprawled before her? This woman who's slept four hours in the last thirty-six? This woman with tears crusting down to her collarbones?

"Yes. Yes I do."

I wipe my face in my shirt, shove everything back into the suitcase, get into the taxi, and hand the driver my address. As we take off into the wheat fields, I breathe and watch the hills roll past. Gazing into miles of sloping wheat, I fantasize about sand-pipers flying en masse—sandpipers momentarily abandoning the whole project of finding clams in sand, of appearing to chase the waves, of oscillation. I imagine them rising up from the beach, somehow moving as a unified company, somehow aware of where to go despite dozens of bodies in such close proximity. I turn to watch the road sprawling in front of us and imagine what it would feel like to expand my speckled wings and know exactly where I need to go.

Part Three

Retrograde Direct Station

The celestial body remains static in preparation for movement; energy unleashed, perhaps unsettling, perhaps revolutionary, perhaps devastating.

Wilma

Your Reading For: December 30, 2013

Welcome back to This Place, sweet Ram! While the holiday festivities this year may only serve to add to your estrangement, remember the circuitous nature of the Wheel of Fortune—what goes up must come down and vice-versa. You cannot know how it feels to be at the top without knowing how it feels at the bottom.

This should've happened sooner. I've been home for two weeks. I've seen all the relatives. I've seen the parade of holiday casseroles and potato bakes and cakes on kitchen countertops. I've hiked over mounds of snow and made flurry angels with Donny in the front yard and fishtailed my father's truck around the highway in two snowstorms. I've been traipsing through my hometown on a daily basis, peering through restaurant and coffee shop windows, seeing the past played out against the present like a film projector, leaving me stricken and afloat. With all this aimless strolling, I should've run into Wilma, or, at least someone, sooner. Wilma is my father's second cousin whom he refers to as "Woozy Wilma." Wilma makes life-sized cloth dolls and plays the mandolin. Wilma chain-smokes and makes her own dresses and, according to my father, used to make cookies for the church bake sale that would invariably have one of her long white-blonde hairs in them. Wilma also likes to shop for discount Russell Stover chocolates at the downtown pharmacy—where I also happen to be today.

After hours of the usual wandering, I decide to loiter and warm up in the pharmacy where I unsuspectingly walk right into Wilma's arms.

Upon stomping through the glass doors, she sees me before I see her and she runs to me, willowy arms and hair outstretched, and gathers me up before I realize who it is that has wrapped their arms around me.

"Oh honey—" she bellows.

Tall woman, long white hair, the smell of cigarettes and—

". . . Wilma?" I say to her right shoulder.

"Shhh . . . darling. Don't say a word."

". . . Okay."

She holds me, rocking me back and forth next to the cough lozenges, Bing Crosby crooning above us. Even though my father has ridiculed and gossiped about Wilma for years—the creepy dolls, the mandolin performances at family reunions, the hairy church cookies—I can feel myself gearing up to bawl, somehow safe and vulnerable in her arms, and I seize up before the deluge sets in.

How did she know to wrap me up like some lost babe? It must've been written all over my face—this alienation, this afloat feeling, this sorrow. Or maybe Wilma's brilliant and intuitive. Sensitive. Caring. I didn't really know her. She hadn't come to any sort of family gathering for years, nearly shunned for her eccentric ways. The last time (and one of the only times) I'd seen her was at my mother's funeral where she'd merely grabbed my elbow and frowned.

Wilma pulls me away from her and keeps me at arm's length as I hold my breath, trying not to fall apart in yet another public space, in yet another near-stranger's arms.

"Courtney. This is tough—I know."

I nod and she thrusts me back into her embrace and whispers into my hair, "You just have to pretend that your mother went to Hawaii. She's in Hawaii! She's in a better place, sweetheart. Think of it—*Hawaii*." And she rocks me back and forth as my estrangement evaporates. I can nearly hear it singe into the atmosphere like water on hot blacktop.

. . . I should pretend my mother went to Hawaii?

It is now not my sorrow that I must mute but wild rage. Because if my mother was really in Hawaii, I could *call* her and ask her why the hell she moved to Hawaii. I could call and scream at her, weep to her, beg her to return. Actually, if my mother was in Hawaii, I wouldn't be mad—I'd be baffled. Why would she move to Hawaii beyond the obvious reasons of surf, sun, and scenery? But regardless of the reasons—I could ask her questions, try to understand, get the story as to why she left. And maybe she could explain her reasons for this strange and unexpected choice— maybe she met a man at the casino and he seduced and persuaded her to move to Hawaii and into his bungalow. Or maybe she gambled all her money away and wanted to start over; move somewhere and waitress, leave her children and forget the past. Or maybe she had a mental break and decided she needed a place to heal, a place to regroup. Or maybe she just wanted a vacation and decided to stay. But most important, if my mother was truly in Hawaii, not only could I talk to her but I could *visit*. I could show up on her doorstep and demand that she tell me why she left. I could slip notes underneath her door seeking answers. I could throw pebbles at her window from the sidewalk until I saw her face peek out from behind a curtain. Or I could just ring the doorbell and I'm sure she'd let me in.

But how could I engage in some delusion about my mother being in Hawaii when I can't even quell my own doubts about the workings of the universe? How could I dare to imagine my mother somewhere in Hawaii when I don't even know if she *exists* anymore?

I break loose from Wilma's embrace and smooth my jacket. Wilma dabs her eyes, mascara adrift, and I feel my rage rise and subside.

As we stand there, boots soaked, noses red and frozen, faces chapped, I can understand thinking of Hawaii as heaven, the afterlife, someplace better. Hawaii is probably warm and humid and sunny. Hawaii is far enough away from This Place to be exciting but not alienating. Hawaii probably seems like a fabulous place to go when you think about death in the depths of a midwestern winter.

I look at Wilma's fragile face; her long, thin nose; her fairy-like hair.

"Wilma . . . I can—that would be great if she was in Hawaii. Thank you."

She grins.

We hug one more time and depart—her to the candy aisle and me right back out the door and onto the icy sidewalk. As darkness settles upon the deserted downtown streets and I walk back to my father's truck, I fantasize about plumeria and hibiscus, about palm trees and pineapples, about sea breeze and sunshine. I climb into the driver's seat, frigid pleather snapping beneath me, gaze at the slick blacktop and imagine her being a plane ride away, her voice on the end of a phone line, her handwriting scrawled across a post-card, *Wish you were here!*

I feel myself grow frantic, the deluge whirling—*Where is my mother?* Was she somewhere sunny and humid like Hawaii? Was she somewhere dark and cold like this Wisconsin night? Could she even *be* somewhere? A physical place? Where did she exist now? If at all?

I exhale, my breath a whimper.

I don't know—I don't know where she is, if she is.

Shoving the key into the ignition, I twist it, listen to the engine turn over, and wish that my mother really was sunbathing on Oahu.

Later that night, I sprawl on my bed to read the spiral-bound journal I created when I was a teenager that outlined my natal chart. I look at my handwritten notes—*Sun in the eleventh house of Aries, Moon in the tenth house of Aquarius, Venus in the twelfth house of Venus,* and so on. I read my notes about the relationships between the planets. *Easy flow between the Moon and Venus, tension between Mercury and Neptune . . .* I read through the challenges and opportunities outlined for growth and expansion. I read about the woman the sky says I could be and I cannot recognize myself in these pages. Who is this person outlined in this notebook?

I don't know . . .

I cannot recognize myself outside of these pages either—Who was that woman falling apart in Wilma's arms? Who is this woman aimlessly roaming around her hometown? What is she looking for?

The same thing she was looking for a year ago . . .

I stare at my handwriting from years past as despair whirls within me. I'm nothing more than a sieve, dribbling my emotions onto whatever I encounter, a weeping young woman wearing her dead mother's clothing. Who am I beyond my mother's death? Who am I without her in my orbit?

I slap the notebook shut, throw it underneath my bed, hurl myself up from the bed and pace. To the window, to the door, and back again. I don't know where she is or if she can even *be* anywhere. To the window, door, and back. I don't know who I am without her. To the window—

To the closet.

Pulling the door open, I walk into everything I abandoned in August as I haphazardly ran out the door and across the country. My mother's sundresses and sweaters lie strewn across the floor, books splayed out as though they had attempted to fly and crashed, shoes and scarves pepper the entire mess while an overflowing box of my mother's swimming suits sits untouched in the corner.

I go to it and open the box, impulsivity throbbing through me. Despite living her entire life in a climate where it's only legitimate beach weather twenty percent of the year, my mother owned beachwear as though it were an essential nutrient needed for survival, just below food and shelter.

Given this, my mother should've been in spectacular health.

The only thing I do know is that after years of sunbathing in the driveway or beside a green lake, my mother and I were going to visit the beaches we fantasized about the year she died. I know that we planned to leave This Place and visit literal Deep Ends together—the Adriatic and Baltic Seas. I know that the last moment we held on to one another as healthy, whole women we had planned to meet beside the sea, away from This Place. I know that my mother had said she wanted to be spread in the lake but that the urn wouldn't budge. And in this moment, in the midst of what feels like a retrograde, where certainty has vanished, I want to take her and put her in the turquoise seas we had planned to visit. I want to take her to literal Deep Ends, to take her away from This Place and do what we planned.

Plunging my hand into the box, I pull out a hideous, floral-patterned one-piece swimming suit circa 1992. I stick it on over my clothing, waddle to the bathroom, and look in the mirror.

I'm a flower sausage.

I peel the suit off, take the box to my bed and start to lay each piece out one by one. A green spangled bikini . . . A purple and gold suit . . . That zebra-striped bikini . . .

I turn the box upside-down and shake it. The suits fall with a sigh. I strip off my clothing, pick up the zebra suit's top, lace it around my arms, tie it together in the back, and pull the bottoms up.

I look down at the bra cups laying on my own chest, round and unfilled, like haute couture armor, and decide it: We're going to go there this summer, she and I. I'll take the ashes and put her there. I stand up straight and feel the suit's polyester soft against my skin. Because I know she wanted to go. Because maybe that's the only thing I do know. Because the urn was soldered shut.

Because there has to be a reason she left me with all of these swimming suits.

Our Stuff

Your Reading For: February 17, 2014
    Young Aries! This is a struggle for you, isn't it?
You cannot rely on static moments. Everything is
in constant movement. Do not cling to stability
thinking it will remain—it won't.

This is Pit overtime—Donny's calling again. He's been down there since early February, but this time he hasn't secluded himself because of grief or our mother or watching *Titanic* on repeat—he's down there because of Paige. She's decided to go off after she graduates and work at a dude ranch or at a national park out West or teach English in Ukraine for a year. She's decided that she wants nothing to do with engagement rings or wedding cake toppers or Donny. She's decided they need to find better people, that they're not right for each other, that it really has to do with her and not with him.

She dumped him a week before Valentine's Day and he's been calling me every day since. He calls to plot how to get her back, to beg me to ask the I Ching what to do, to ask the I Ching if they'll get back together, to ask the I Ching what she's thinking, and to let me decipher his sobs through the phone line.

When I'd told Donny about the I Ching years before, he'd only cackled in return, "You're doing *what?* You're looking at dingalings? Oh, the I Ching? Don't you mean ah-ah-choo?" Etc. But in his time of crisis, he's learned to pronounce it. *EEE-ching.* He tells me, "I need to know what the eee-ching thinks . . ."

The I Ching usually just tells him to disengage from his emotions and take no action; let the Sage do its work and all will be resolved. Which is usually what the I Ching says.

I'm walking back to my apartment after class and Donny calls me as he's been doing every day between four and five in the afternoon.

I pick up.

"Hi, Donny."

"You gotta look up our stuff, Court."

"What stuff?"

"That natal astrology thingie whatever. For me—and Paige."

"You want me to look at a *synastry* chart for you and Paige?"

"Yeah . . . er, whatever that thing was you did for you and Richard. The relationship chart."

On my own, I'd already astrologically examined their love up and down and I remember that the planets said their relationship was beautiful and magical and possibly made for the long term and that there's no good reason for Donny to see any of it right now.

I try to talk him down—What's the point of doing a chart, Donny? I tell him it's best to let this whole thing be. Remember what the I Ching said? Just relax and try to get your mind off it. Plus? All of this stuff might be useless—I haven't looked at it in a while, Donny.

He pleads. He begs. He tells me that he just wants to know— he just *has* to know.

"Please. Just tell me what it says. I'm not going to get upset."

"You're going to get upset."

"No. I won't. I promise. Just look't it. *Please*, Court."

My apartment is two blocks away.

I tell him to gimme a half-hour and I'll call him back and tell him what it says.

Once home, I put my backpack on the floor, sit at my desk, and pull up an astrology software program to cast their chart. It was as I remembered. Their Sun and Moon are in harmony, Venus and Mars act together positively with just the right amount of se-riousness to hold a relationship together through the influence of Saturn. Marriage markers, trines, and sunshine. All around, it's a harmonious chart that shows a loving relationship between two people that could be together for a long time. There were challeng-ing aspects as well but nothing that couldn't be overcome. As I looked, I fantasized that it was actually an astrological disaster, full of Plutonian funk and Neptunian illusions and Uranus-like ambivalence—the classic signs of a doomed relationship.

But it wasn't.

Dammit.

I call Donny back and listen to the phone ring. Do I tell him all of this? Do I tell him that his nonexistent relationship was sanctified by the planets? Or do I tell him that it's maybe better not to know what could've been with her? Or do I just tell him it's all bogus anyway and not to worry about it?

He picks up.

". . . Well?"

"Donny. It's maybe better for you not to know any of this right now."

He pauses.

"Soooo . . . you're basically telling me, it's good. You're basically telling me we're meant to be, right?"

"No. I don't know. A chart can't tell you whether it's meant to be. Nothing can tell you that. It has to happen in real life. You make all the choices. A chart is just the potential for something to happen, not the promise that it will."

He is quiet.

"Donny . . . I'm really sorry she's gone, but . . . there are some things that maybe only make sense later . . ."

He sniffles and wipes his sleeve against his nose, a muffled rustle.

". . . If I tell you what this chart says it's only going to make you feel worse right now, Donny."

He sighs.

". . . Yeah, maybe you're right. Maybe better not to know what would've been if she was still around."

"I'm sorry, Donny."

"I'm sorry too."

"So . . . what else are you doing today?" I ask.

He tells me about coaching youth hockey and about each of the players as my eyes roam my desk. Random mechanical pencils . . . a half-full coffee cup from this morning . . . a brochure I found at a gas station about invasive plant species . . . a used travel guide to Croatia my mother gave me before I went to Hungary. I pick it up and look through it as Donny tells me about their last game in Stillwater. I skim the map—*Istria, Slavonia, Zagorje, Dubrovnik* . . . I trace the outline of Croatia with my pointer finger. Down the coast, around the Dalmatian shore, up to Zagreb . . .

"Courtney? Are you there?"

I draw my hand back.

"Yes. Yes, Donny. I'm here."

The phone line hums.

"I just booked my tickets for my trip with Mom," I whisper.

I run my finger back along the coast and out into the Adriatic Sea as uncertainty blooms through me.

"Well, how are you gonna get the urn open? You're not gonna try to crack it open there, are you?"

"No, no. I took it to a machine shop over Christmas and they opened it."

"Oh, okay . . . Well, are you excited?" Donny asks.

"Uh . . ."

I let the book fall closed and look out the window, phone still pressed to my ear. My roommates cackle in the kitchen. Snow-covered wheat fields roll outside and my stomach reels as though I were on a sled, sliding up and down those hills.

"I'm not sure," I reply.

". . . What do you mean? It's a vacation! I'd be excited."

"I—I don't know, Donny. I just. I'm gonna go because we said we were going to and she left me a bunch of swimming suits. That's . . . that's all I know. I don't . . . I'm not sure how I feel about it."

"Okay, Court. Well, whatever . . ."

We hang up.

Dishes slam in the kitchen. Liquid splatters—something spilled—my roommates laugh. I slither down onto the carpeted floor, roll onto my back to stare up at the spangled ceiling, and try to find shapes in the sparkles . . . a Charolais cow with an exquisite tail, a monster daisy, two buck teeth. A car drives by, headlights bright, and the glitter transforms. The cow disappears. The daisy grows more grotesque, the buck teeth become bricks, and I think of Linda Goodman setting the table for her lost lover, Robert Brewer, for years after his death. I think of her sleeping outside St.

Patrick's Cathedral awash in belief that her daughter's death was a conspiracy. I think of her nervously picking at her nails outside the CIA headquarters, scratching her brunette hair at the dinner table, and skimming astrology charts before collapsing into bed. Did she wonder as she slept on that sidewalk or as she set Robert's inevitably empty place setting if she was foolish to think that her lover and her daughter were still alive? Did she doubt her belief in the planet's predictions even though she, for many, was a sole interpreter of their messages? She died never having reunited with her daughter or her lover. Were all of the signs there and she refused to look? Or were there no signs at all?

I hold my torso and curl into a ball as the glitter above me morphs again and dissolves into an indistinguishable galaxy. I close my eyes and know that despite this radio silence, despite my woo-woo tokens still being shoved in my closet at home, despite my doubts, the need for a definitive answer—about my mother's whereabouts, about the workings of the universe, about trusting in a larger order—is ever rooted within me.

Vader

Your Reading For: May 4, 2014

Really, young Ram? The universe is not so complicated as to make you constantly guess—we don't engage in such games. If you feel it to be true, then it is. If not, then forget it. There's no need to cry; stand in your truth and trust yourself.

Donny. Will you—talk to me?"
"Sure, I'll talk to you . . . What's wrong?"
"Darth Vader—died."

I had to call Donny. I am balled up on the floor of my friend's bedroom and we are back in The Pit. This is sudden devastation Pit. Erratic, hysterical, lost-my-mind Pit. This is Donny's-time-to-shine-using-his-intuitive-sensitive-empathetic-Pisces-self Pit. This time he is therapist. I am patient.

"What, *what's* wrong?" Donny asks.

"Darth—Vader—*died*," I whisper.

I had just witnessed him fall backward with Luke watching. I had just seen a son promise that he wouldn't leave, a son who bowed his head in devastation. I had witnessed a soul leave a body. A passage. A moment of cosmic significance. A moment of emotional gravity. Someone *died*.

"Wait. Where are you?"

"I'm in—my friend's—bedroom," I reply.

The anniversary of our mother's death, May 4, also happens to be International Star Wars Day. A friend suggested that we watch the *Star Wars* trilogy on the weekend of her death as "a distraction." We watched the original movies, starting with *Star Wars: A*

New Hope on Friday, followed by *The Empire Strikes Back* on Saturday, and then *Return of the Jedi* today, Sunday. Despite the fact that I had just watched Vader wield total viciousness as the henchman of a corrupt empire and chop off his own son's hand and act like an intergalactic jackass, empathy did not escape me. This afternoon as I watched Luke drag his father to safety like his little black-clad bumpkin child and take off his mask to reveal Darth Vader's true, pale, floppy self before he closed his eyes for the final time and fell back into death—*Now, go, my son. Leave me*—I lost it. I wailed. I had to leave the room. I had a meltdown as soon as Luke bowed his head.

Vader's death had catapulted me into The Pit.

I whimper and feel the presence of Donny putting on his calm therapist persona in which he pauses and speaks gently as though he were talking to a distraught toddler bawling on the sidewalk with a skinned knee. "I'm confused, Court. What's goin' on?"

I don't really know what's going on. I'm bawling over *Star Wars*. I'm bawling when I should be cheering Darth Vader's death. I'm bawling because I project my sorrow on everything and have no sense of unbiased reality.

"I watched—*Star Wars* and—Vader died. And—I'm . . . sad."

"Oh—Court. I'm sorry you're sad, but it's okay that Vader died. Vader's evil," he coos.

"No, no—*Vader* had a *soul*. Vader was a human *being*. Or—he was—something, I don't know what he was. But he *died*. And that is *sad*."

I can feel Donny skimming through his college memories of talking with drunk buddies on bathroom floors and coaxing them to safety. I've seen him do this with Bruce, talk to him real sweet and calm and wait out his intoxication to get off the floor or up from the dock. He was pulling the same tactic—though I wasn't intoxicated, just distraught.

"But Court, Vader was *evil*. He had to die."

"Darth Vader had a soul . . ."

"Well." Donny pauses. "He sure did."

Donny gears up to change the subject to something else, anything else, something that doesn't have to do with death or *Star Wars* or souls or a sister he cannot talk down from her hysteria.

"When are you leaving for your trip?"

"A few—weeks."

"Oh, boy. That should be fun."

Donny doesn't talk like this. He's in This Place script mode. He's in replaying-what-he-heard-on-television-when-he-was-eight mode when he says phrases like "sure" and "oh boy" and "you betcha." He's in faker, syrupy, Midwest smooth-everything-over, say-what-you-think-they-want-to-hear mode.

"Where are you going again?"

"I'm going to—Croatia and Bosnia Herzegovina. And Latvia."

". . . You're going to *Bosnia*? What the fuck is in *Bosnia*?"

Script dropped.

"Things . . . lots of things! It's a different place. I don't know! I just wanna see it."

"Aren't there land mines and shit over there?"

"Yes . . . but they're marked. I should be fine. I'm just going to the beach."

"Land mines . . . that's weird shit, man."

Pause. He sighs. Scratches beard. I imagine him looking around the room and spying his video game controller or an open *Sports Illustrated* tossed on the floor or something else more entertaining than this conversation. Donny then gives his standard ending.

"Well, Court, I gotta go. But you're gonna be okay. This is the way the game goes sometimes and you just gotta play it. So, you just keep on. Okay?"

"Okay. I'm gonna be okay. Vader—died. But I'm gonna be okay."

"You're gonna be *better* than okay *because* Vader's dead. Vader was a fucker."

We hang up.

Outside, the *Star Wars* theme plays. My friend and her roommate chatter. Why did my mother die on International Star Wars Day? Why did she die on a day that celebrates a movie series that centers on invisible forces permeating and binding the universe together? On the day that celebrates a movie series rife with unseen magical energies? Am I once again reading into my surroundings, trying to suss out what I hope to see? Or is this a sign staring me straight in the face?

I haul myself up from the floor and wonder how I can ever be sure of anything.

But it is not until over a month later, as I sit crammed into an airplane seat flying over the Atlantic, in my very own pit again—no Donny to call, no mother to bawl to, no sense of internal fortitude, divinatory tools all left at home—that I take any decisive action.

The density of my misgivings nearly squashing me, cramped and restless, I fling my blanket off me, unbuckle my seatbelt, peel my legs out from the row, and stumble to the lavatory.

I stare into the cloudy mirror and contemplate what I could possibly do in an airplane bathroom, hours away from landing, to gain any clarity.

I have looked for signs and not looked for signs. I have clung to crystal quartz points and burned so much sage my roommates complained and tracked Pluto's transits again and again. I have pondered my own uncertainty for months, but I have not asked for any guidance or help.

I look at the floor.

I look at the door.

I look back at the floor.

I slap my hands together and sink to the greasy rubber floor, vacuum toilet hissing behind me, close my eyes, and ask in a whisper, "Dear . . . whoever is there—can you—please—if you can—during this trip—send me a . . . sign? A sign. Please send me a sign. I can't do this anymore. I can't wonder or not know. So please, I would like to know if there is some—kind of force or, you know, energy around everything. Send me a sign so that I can know if my mother is—somewhere. So that I can—know. For sure."

I pause.

I am an imbecile.

I am the most ridiculous person alive squatting on the floor of this icky little bathroom praying. I'm *praying* when I don't even know if I believe in anything. Why am I asking for a sign after my mother told me she doesn't believe? When I have ignored some signs and read signs into innocuous symbols and occurrences?

Despite my supposed knowledge and interest in the Deep End, why am I asking for a sign when I am too disconnected from my own sense of truth to even know how to interpret anything?

"And—if you—do send me a sign—can it be something—recognizable—certain—something I won't—be able to dispute?"

My right foot goes numb.

"And if nothing happens—if nothing occurs, I'll know. I'll know she's not there and there's nothing there and I'll see it and believe it . . . Okay—I'm, I'm done. Thank you." I try to stand up and stumble, my left elbow careening into the slick sink.

"Ouch—"

I regain my footing, turn the lock to green, and walk back into the cabin. Reading lights dot the dark interior as I walk to my seat.

Throwing the thin fleece blanket on, I tuck the fabric tight under myself and close my eyes, a chrysalis in a cocoon. I imagine this is what trust feels like—to be bundled in belief, bound solid by faith. I imagine this is what it feels like to be your own pendulum, a singular unit of guidance moving forward and gliding through the atmosphere.

Split

Your Reading For: June 3, 2014
    Yes, this will sound contradictory, but release
your grip on needing to know.

Imagine this postcard: a ground shot of Croatia's seaside city, Split. A white marble boardwalk lines the sea. Latte-drinking locals populate the outdoor cafés. Seagulls swoop. Palm trees thick at the waist tremble. A busker sings about heartache and rum behind an electric beat. Tan tourists with sunglasses and shopping bags stroll. Heat reflects off their sunglasses, off the boardwalk, off the sea. It's picturesque. Charming. If you squint and look closer, you'll see a young woman in the distance—head drooped, shoulders slumped. A jar in the crook of her left arm, a map sprawled loose in her other hand. She's a paradox of a visitor—sullen in sunglasses and black sarong among her vibrant contemporaries.

Here's another postcard: a shot of Split's main beach, Bačvice. All sand and surf and sunshine. Mothers hold their toddlers' pudgy hands as the children dip their toes into the sea. Women lounge beneath yellow umbrellas. Bronzed sunbathers glazed with oil lie on dark towels, sunglasses perched on their noses. Teenage girls in impossibly tiny bikinis watch teenage boys shove one another around in the water. Aquamarine waves are captured in mid-roll and mid-recede. Squint again and you'll see the same young woman in mid-stride with head hung, carrying that jar, the map now rolled up in her hands.

If you could follow that woman, you'd find her walking past Bačvice, past the toddlers and sunbathers, past the tourists and trinkets, past the ice-cream stands and seaside bars, past coves and

177

shallow waters, and you'd find her standing before a vacant patch of deep plummeting seaside. You'd find her unrolling a towel and sitting at the foot of it, the jar clammy in her hand. You'd see her sit with that jar in her hands for minutes upon minutes. She longs. Longs not to feel like a caricature of a traveler—a woman vacationing with a mustard jar. Longs not to feel absurd taking a trip with her mother without her mother. Longs to be her own compass, to find guidance not from desperately clinging but from an inner fortitude. Longs to know that her mother *is*.

You'd see her breathe with purpose, to break out of her fog, to stay steady, belly expanding and contracting. She unscrews the lid, shakes a gray substance into her hands, and stares into the mass. If her thoughts could be visible, you'd see her reeling over the ambiguity of her mother's remains, lost in the mystery surrounding a woman she once thought she knew so well. She stares and stares and imagines all the substances her mother could be. *French flour . . . Caribbean sand . . . February-era snow . . .*

The young woman stands, holding the powder in her hands.

Ground aspirin, copy machine toner . . .

The young woman walks to the water.

Powdered milk, loose gunpowder . . .

The water splashes against her ankles, *talcum powder*, against her knees, *ground crystal quartz*, up to her thighs, *raw sugar*, until she is waist-deep in the water.

Holding the ashes above her, she closes her eyes and whispers, *Thank you for being my mother.*

She lets the ashes fall into the water and with each wave, they dissipate further into the water, until they are turquoise, until they are sand, until they are sea. Staring into the expanse before her, she walks backwards until she can sit and wonders if her mother really could be anywhere or be anything. *This sand? This sea?* She wonders what streams and currents her mother swims in, if any. *This one right in front of me?* She wonders if her mother is guiding her. *How else did I make it here?* She wonders if she were to fully embrace the Deep End, if she were to charge into these waters, if she would find her mother there. *Would I?* And if she were to stand up and charge in, how would she know? What form would she take? Who would she be?

Snap a picture of that young woman and you'll see that it's me.

I look into the water to see if I can spot the mound that is my mother, but all I see is her as the sand, her as the water, her as the sea. I turn to look at the horizon, the sun hot on my shoulders, and if I could write a tagline to the postcard of me sitting in the Adriatic it would be this: *My mother is Croatia.*

Sarajevo

Your Reading For: June 7, 2014
   This is supposed to be a vacation, right? Trust
that if there is a sign to be seen, you will see it.

Four days later, after watching the sun crawl over the Croatian seascape and disappear once again, after a bus ride along Croatia's coast and over the border of Bosnia Herzegovina, after a bag of apples and Bajadera candy, after walking through Mostar's romantic landscape of Ottoman bridges and bullet-ravaged buildings, after arriving in Sarajevo and traipsing around lost for the past two hours, I stand at the entrance of the local zoo in northern Sarajevo.

I stare at the zoo's cloverleaf emblem and feel the vast space between this charming red-roofed city of Austro-Hungarian architecture and its visible war-torn past ring wide within me. Standing between evidence of its palpable past and ardent efforts to rebuild, I am timid, uncertain. I adjust the strap on my backpack, listen to my mother's ashes roll around the bottom, and walk through the zoo's main entrance of green painted steel. Oak trees line the zoo's perimeter and inside it's a children's oasis—a giant fiberglass mushroom looms, providing shelter from the sun for visitors, an ice-cream stand plays music, and primary-colored wooden benches dot the paths. I pull out a fist-sized souvenir teddy bear with SARAJEVO printed across its chest that I bought at a gas station and stick it in the crook of my arm, buy an ice-cream cone, and stroll along the zoo's rock path. I lick the ice cream and watch swans gliding on dark waters; a pheasant cackles in a cage. I bite into the cone and stare at meerkats preoccupied with the innards of a tree stump. I lick melted ice cream off my hand and spot a red fox with black socks for feet as caramel-colored Highland cattle look out from behind their shaggy hair. I start to eat the cone and stop before an exhibit housing creatures unrecognizable to me. Muscular arms stack on top of their impossibly long bamboo legs. *What are they?* The creatures lounge on the dirt-floor enclosure like leisurely bachelors sprawled on couches. None of them roam. I eat the rest of the cone and stand there for a solid half-hour absorbed in my own obtuseness, waiting for recognition to waft over me, until a raindrop falls on my neck.

And then another on my shoulder.

My arm.

My right hand.

The sidewalk begins to speckle.

I look at the dark sky.

It begins to pour.

Dumbfounded, I stand there watching the mystery creatures stare at the other zoo guests leaving in droves. My arms glisten. Parents pull their wailing children along. Teenagers are shooed out and sprint from their nooks near the swans; hickeys bright on their necks. The ice-cream man drags his cart inside the closed café for refuge. I pull my umbrella out, cast one last glance at the animals, and accidentally drop my souvenir bear onto the cage's gravel lining. Thunder rolls. I pick the bear up and run with everyone else out of the zoo's gates to a restaurant across the street.

The formerly idle restaurant now buzzes in the late afternoon with zoo guests who've taken shelter. The single waiter on duty slouches and sighs behind the hostess stand as he looks across the covered outdoor seating area now crawling with squirming children, exasperated parents, teenagers creating towers out of the salt and pepper shakers on the table, elderly patrons waiting patiently, and me staring at the dining room's rustic wooden interior and running my finger along the table's deep cedar grooves.

I order an espresso and turn the image of those creatures over in my mind.

The espresso arrives. *Those creatures . . .* I try my best at saying "thank you." *Hvala.* The server walks away. *Their legs like sticks.* Stare at my coffee. *Just lying there.* Take a sip. *I have no idea what they were . . .* I fold my napkin into a swan and flap its wings, a baby at the next table gawking at me.

Within an hour, the clouds scurry on and my fellow zoo visitors vacate the restaurant.

I leave a coin for my coffee and follow them.

As I walk back toward the city center, the call to prayer radiates throughout the city, and with each block I think of all that I cannot know—from those creatures at the zoo to the messages of these Bosnian billboards lining this street, to the truth bubbling behind the hearsay and stoic faces of my homeland, to the exact meaning of the planets above and the questions I carry—and I wait for that sense of dread to unfurl, for my hands to shake, for anxiety to swell, but, somehow, with each block I remain steady. With each sidewalk segment up the hill to my bed, despite the vast unknown surrounding me, I can still find my way home.

Forty-eight hours later, I wash my hands inside the Sarajevo airport. Pink iridescent soap undulating in my hands, ticket to Riga in my back pocket, ashes shaking like a rattle in my backpack, as a woman wearing a Baby Björn and carrying a sleeping infant against her chest begins to wash her hands next to me and I reali—

Kangaroos. They were kangaroos.

Viktorijas

Your Reading For: June 10, 2014
Little Ram! Now is the time! Sing your part!

Hours later, I arrive in Riga, Latvia. Standing at the airport bus stop, the sun backlights the airport sign, LIDOSTA RĪGA AIRPORT, and I look across the empty parking lot. It's nine at night but still light out. Lime-green taxis arrive and depart. Suitcase rollers get stuck and pulled out of sidewalk gaps. Pigeons gather near the overflowing garbage cans and I remember the moments I have stood at this exact bus stop in years past—teeth chattering, the sign covered in snow; sopping wet, the sign glistening with rain; tired and groggy, the sign glowing red in the night. As I stare at the familiar sign, my comfort slowly dissolves to anguish.

Bus twenty-two bound for the city center approaches, appearing out of a sprawling green field and rounding the curve up to the bus stop. The father and daughter holding hands next to me bicker about the Laima chocolates he refused to buy for her. The daughter, no more than six, asks repeatedly, why? *Kāpēc?* Why? She wants it—*es gribu šokolādi* . . . Behind us, two men whisper in Russian. I had always loved listening to Russian—I didn't understand a word, but I liked the buzzing and lilting, the clusters of consonants, the long vowels. The bus approaches and the little girl keeps ranting and all I can hear are the consonants cutting above the men's whispers and she keeps asking *why* and I am all raw nerve.

Despite this trip, despite taking my mother with me, despite all of the *worry* and *oscillation* and *contemplation* of the past year, despite praying on the sticky floor of an airplane bathroom and trying to trust that an answer will come, I haven't progressed forward—I've only come back to a place I already know. Why am I here staring at this airport again? Is *this* the sign? The sign of total stagnation? The sign that I've just been running to what is most familiar rather than finding my own sense of guidance? The sign that there are no more signs to be seen?

I squeeze the straps of my backpack, remorse running through me. Why did I come here with a jar of ashes? My mother and I wanted to come here to visit this place *together*—What was the point of me being here now? I'm a joke of a visitor, a daughter on a vacation "with" her mother who happens to be dead.

Lugging suitcases and duffel bags, the dozen of us waiting for the bus meander toward it. I stand in line as the father promises his daughter that she'll get a chocolate once they're home. I step onto the bus as the men whispering Russian grow more heated in their conversation. I swipe my pass, shuffle to the back of the bus, grab a railing, and decide that I am an unequivocal moron. Should I even go to the sea to spread her ashes? Did she even want to be put here? Hadn't she just wanted to come to Latvia with me because I'd wanted her to? Would she have come here of her own accord?

The bus churns and we veer away from the airport, past the Maxima XXX supermarket and the Rimi grocery store and the Spice hypermarket, toward the rolling Daugava River, and over the bridge. I watch the scene scroll past—couples hold hands and walk past the movie theater. Shoppers carry bags of vegetables and bread past soot-stained buildings. Teenagers loiter on street corners, smoking cigarettes and checking their cell phones. We drive up 13 Janvāra Street. I get off on Gertrūdes Street and walk the ten minutes toward the city center where I'm sleeping on a friend's couch, ashes chittering in my backpack as though they are keeping me company, speaking a secret language the whole way, regret thrumming through me with each step.

The next day, I wake up and stare at the crack running diagonally across the ivory-colored ceiling of my friend's apartment and debate what to do with the day.

My friend left a key and a note for me—*Come and go as you please.*

I did come all this way.

I might as well take a walk.

I grab my backpack and go.

I spend the morning meandering Riga's streets in a vacant haze, passively consuming my surroundings. I amble past women in long skirts pushing prams, businessmen urgently walking past, gray-haired women rolling their groceries behind them in plaid carts, and I remember living here years ago and walking these same streets awash with wonder. I walk and remember the bakeries and the bowls of gray peas with salted pork fat and lying in bed at night, my stomach in knots from the grease. I walk past theaters and stare up at their box-office facades and remember the hours I spent in the dark saturated in confusion and awe at these plays in foreign languages. I remember wondering how to be comfortable with the uncomfortable, how to chart the unknown around me.

I walk through the groomed city park of flowers and canals and remember the times I came to sit and watch ducks glide on murky waters. I remember my comfort at the familiar red carnations and green mallards.

I walk through the immense Central Market housed in four old German Zeppelin airship hangars and remember my language stumbles, my embarrassment over trying to ask for lettuce or eggs and walking back to my apartment empty-handed. I walk through the fish section and stare into a bucket of eels, like the one that had so unsettled me years earlier as its inhabitants flopped and slithered. I pass by a flower stand and buy a handful of lilacs—the kind my mother and I used to cut, pulling over on the side of the road in Wisconsin when we saw a blooming rural bush. I stick my face into the flowers and breathe in their familiar tang.

I leave the market and find myself at the train station. I stop and stare at the arrivals and departures board as travelers rush past me each way: RĪGA—OGRE. RĪGA—CĒSIS. RĪGA—JELGAVA. RĪGA—MAJORI. Majori is a seaside town where I'd gone once before in the middle of winter. The train leaves in ten minutes. *I came all this way* . . . A woman running with a stroller nearly clips me. Platform four. The intercom comes on announcing a route closure. The train leaves in nine minutes. A group of Estonian tourists stroll past. Platform four. I stare and watch the clock. The train leaves in eight minutes . . . *I came all this way* . . . Seven minutes.

I stare.

Six minutes.

I run to the platform, lilac flowers trailing past me.

In Majori, the wind blows, picking up dust and throwing it north through the quaint city center. I walk past stalls selling amber jewelry, Dinamo Riga hockey apparel, and matryoshka nesting dolls. Keychains on display clink in the wind. I walk past the stall operators who throw tarps over their wares as the sky grows darker. Tourists in plastic ponchos and sneakers laugh at their ensembles billowing in the wind. Skinny high-school sweethearts hold hands and dangerously take shelter under elm trees as the sky turns darker while white-haired couples drink espresso underneath trembling umbrellas. I keep walking and despite the gusts and gloomy sky, I take a sharp left to the sea—any street headed north will take you there.

Because I came all this way.

I might as well see it.

I walk through six blocks of residential housing, the sky growing darker with each passing block, and gaze at the ornate houses lining the streets. *Why is it always raining on this trip?* I imagine Soviet leaders of years past in full regalia mowing their lawns, trimming the shrubs, and cleaning the drainpipes, up to their elbows in pulverized, greasy foliage. The wind blows. Trim lawns and elm trees shiver. As I walk, I imagine who lives in these houses now— maybe Russian millionaires or Estonian architects. The wind dies with an audible sigh. Maybe renowned Latvian poets who plant cabbages and carrots in the backyard. Or maybe Siberian tech—I look up and read the street sign. *Viktorijas Iela.*

I stop. The wind blows again. Dried leaves and dust whirl past.

That's my mother's name. Victoria.

Viktorijas Iela.

I didn't know this street existed. I didn't know *Viktorijas* was a Latvian name. I didn't know—

Victoria Street. I'm on my mother's street.

The wind gusts again—I look to the right.

A wooden platform leading to the sea stretches out before me.

I put my hood up and follow it.

Mist descends on the beach. Walking across the platform, I reach the wet sand and look out before me.

I stick the lilacs in my backpack, take my sandals off, roll my jeans up to my knees, and walk the hundred yards to the sea. Storm clouds stir in the distance, billowing dark. I take the ashes out of my backpack. I wade into the sea, twist the lid, and turn the jar over.

Thank you for guiding me to your path . . .

Wind catches the ashes and propels them away from me as though the particles were racing one another. The ashes careen into the water, sink to the bottom, and with each wave they grow more indistinguishable until she is the sand, she is the sea, she is the tide.

I look across the horizon.

Mist crescendos to rain.

Waves undulate around my ankles. I look at the empty jar in my hands and think of it again. *Viktorijas Iela.* I had been led to Victoria Street.

It was a sign. A literal sign. The most clear sign possible.

And then, in my mind, the music starts.

Cue the clarinet! Get that tambourine ready! Make sure those harmonies are in order!

I hear the opening lines—the clarinet cooing, that tambourine quivering in anticipation of its big moment. I hear Karen Carpenter's voice—she's singing about optimism and hope. She's singing with anticipation for the future. She's singing about a new beginning and yes, it *is* true! We've only just begun! The clarinet trills. Richard Carpenter chimes in and I imagine my mother's voice singing backup, cooing along.

Lightning snaps and shutters. My hood slides off my head. Sweater-wearing walkers, huffing joggers, and hooded men swaying near the shoreline with metal detectors start to retreat toward a beer tent. Wind swells the tent's canvas siding out like a prairie chicken's air sacs during courtship. I look back and watch it. *That thing looks like it's going to fall over . . .*

But we're still singing!

Karen's singing! My mother's singing! Richard's singing! I'm singing! *And this is the path I ended up on . . .*

I'm on Victoria Street.

The empty jar fills with water. The sky cracks and moans.

I look back to the sea. Thunder reverberates. It starts to pour, a burst showerhead. The sand twitches with rain as the song glides along with those gleeful notes, that joyous melody, those lo—

Let's get the hell out of here.

Hours later, after the storm has passed, I take the train back to Riga. Holding the empty jar in my hands, I see myself swinging, a pendulum dancing, the weight of uncertainty lifted. The countryside glides by as a train attendant looks at my ticket. A couple behind me whispers in Lithuanian and the answers broadcasts from within me—*yes, yes, yes*—I am the pendulum. I am the guide. And she is here.

Part Four

Post-Retrograde Shadow

The celestial body moves forward; shake, awake, heal.

Plunge

Your Reading For: August 1, 2014
    Welcome home! Take it from your mother—
sometimes a new swimwear purchase really can
make you feel brand new.

With my mother's urn hollow in my arms, we are again anchored in the middle of the lake. Silent behind sunglasses, Bruce sits at the pontoon wheel with the mid-afternoon sun bright above us.

The waves dip and churn as Donny stumbles at the edge of the boat with the rest of our mother's ashes cupped in his hands. Regaining his footing, he throws his arms open. Released, they rise and fall before disappearing into the quivering lake.

The pontoon rocks up and down.

I watch Donny watch the water.

To the fishing boats plodding along with their lines out, the boaters sitting shotgun with Coronas in their hands, and the canoe paddlers gliding along, it must've looked like my brother was tossing birdseed or glitter. It must've looked like he was celebrating.

Donny turns around to look at me, the air heavy with humidity, as I think, *Our mother is confetti.*

Later that evening as the sun begins to set, turning the sky autumnal, I change into a bathing suit and walk down the steep steps leading to the lake. As I descend, I see Paige and Donny sitting on the dock, their toes skimming the lake's surface. Lanky oaks and honeysuckle shrubs grow lush on either side of the stairs. I step onto the wooden platform extending into the water twenty yards long.

Donny and Paige turn around and wave.

I wave back and signal that I'm going to jump. They scoot over making room for my leap. I look down at my toes. I look at the end of the dock.

I inhale.

I run across the wooden slats, my feet thumping beneath me as the dock shudders that same shudder it did when I was a child, when there was something enchanting about the mysterious uncertainty of its structure, its apparent sturdiness that still wavered under your step.

I run past the boat lift. I run past Donny and Paige. I run past the steel poles that flank the dock's perimeter. I run past the dock and push off from those raw wooden edges, the crude lumber's prickle pressing into my bare feet with a sting. I kick my right leg in front of me, left leg tucking behind me in the air. Arms drawn close, my body rises and for a mere moment, I feel as though I am levitating. The lake undulates dark and green beneath me. I feel my body cascade into its glossy expanse, toes touching the water. I close my eyes and envision a woman in motion as my ankles immerse, a woman gliding into the new as my knees and thighs submerge, a woman buoyant and alive as my arms and shoulders go under, a woman reborn as my head dunks and resurfaces.

That woman . . .

I inhale, wipe the water from my eyes, shake my head, water splattering, and stare back at the dock.

That woman is me.

Acknowledgments

Infinite gratitude to:

The editors of the following journals where previous portions of the manuscript have appeared: *The Masters Review*, *Black Warrior Review*, *River Teeth*, *Storm Cellar Quarterly*, and *Sweet*.

Raphael Kadushin and the University of Wisconsin Press for their support and belief in my work. I am beyond grateful.

Anna Banks, Mary Clearman Blew, Scott Slovic, and Alexandra Teague for their advice, patience, and encouragement in working with me on this manuscript.

My colleagues and classmates at the University of Idaho and the University of California, Santa Cruz, for their support and cheer.

The following institutions that provided time and space to write: the Writing in the Wild Fellowship at the University of Idaho, the Regent's Fellowship at the University of California, Santa Cruz, and the Great Basin Writer's Residency hosted by Dave and Roberta Moore—most sincere thanks all around.

My family and friends of the Upper Midwest and elsewhere: a thankfulness beyond words.

Cody R. Brown for listening, reading, and sharing.

My mother, Victoria, for the honor of telling a part of her story and being her daughter.